PRAISE FOR *THE NOTICER RETURNS*

"*The Noticer Returns* is a magical story that will change how you look at life."

> — Winston Groom, *New York Times* best-selling author of *Forrest Gump*

"I read everything he writes again and again. Andy Andrews is, quite simply, my favorite author."

> — Margaret Kelly, CEO, RE/MAX

"The amazing principles Andy Andrews reveals in his books are a large part of the success we have been able to achieve as a hospital system. In *The Noticer Returns* be sure to pay particular attention to his 'Secret Philosophy of Extreme Achievement.' That one nugget of wisdom continues to produce outstanding results for our employees—personally and professionally—every single day."

> — John Heer, president/CEO, North Mississippi Health Services; and the world's only three-time Baldrige Award recipient

"Parenting . . . creating a profitable business from scratch . . . even a mind-blowing perspective on dealing with Alzheimer's and death . . . *The Noticer Returns* is a book you and I will purchase by the case. Let's give this book to as many people as we can and begin changing the world right now!"

> — Tim Hudson, Atlanta Braves pitcher

"Andy Andrews is America's greatest storyteller since Mark Twain and perhaps our most interesting teacher since Robin Williams played John Keating in the movie *Dead Poets Society*. *The Noticer Returns* is another in his long line of winners."

> — Robert Mayes, president, Columbia Southern University

"If Andy Andrews lived in England, the queen would have knighted him by now. Andy's books—*all* of his books—are just that good!"

— Louie Anderson, comedian and actor

"*The Noticer Returns* is better than *great* and has the power to cement the direction of your family for generations. Andy Andrews has become the wise master of storytelling."

— Paul Westphal, former Lakers All-Star and NBA head coach

"With *The Noticer Returns* it has become clear that Andy Andrews owns this genre. Once again he has created a satisfying blend of life-changing principles with a fantastic storyline. Andy has singlehandedly turned the 'inspirational novel' into an art form."

— Brenda Warner, best-selling author and speaker

"Parents, coaches, employers, and employees . . . drop what you're doing and read this book today! Andy Andrews reveals uncommon wisdom in a common sense kind of way. *The Noticer Returns* is a guidebook to the life you've always wanted for your family."

— Kurt Warner, Super Bowl champion quarterback and NFL broadcaster

"Andy Andrews is my favorite author . . . my very favorite."

— Robert Morris, founding senior pastor, Gateway Church

"If C. S. Lewis were alive today, his favorite author would be Andy Andrews."

— Sandi Patty, vocal artist, winner of more than 25 Grammy and Dove awards

The

NOTICER
RETURNS

The
NOTICER
RETURNS

Sometimes You Find Perspective,
and Sometimes Perspective Finds You

ANDY ANDREWS

W PUBLISHING GROUP

AN IMPRINT OF THOMAS NELSON

Published in Nashville, Tennessee, by W Publishing Group. W Publishing is a registered trademark of Thomas Nelson, Inc.

Thomas Nelson, Inc., titles may be purchased in bulk for educational, business, fund-raising, or sales promotional use. For information, please e-mail SpecialMarkets@ThomasNelson.com.

Library of Congress Cataloging-in-Publication Data

Andrews, Andy, 1959–
  The noticer returns : sometimes you find perspective, and sometimes perspective finds you / Andy Andrews.
     pages cm
  Includes bibliographical references and index.
  ISBN 978-0-7852-3145-5 (hardcover : alk. paper) 1. Conduct of life. 2. Perspective (Philosophy) 3. Insight. I. Title.
  BJ1597.A527 2013
  170'.44—dc23   2013013479

Printed in the United States of America

13 14 15 16 17 RRD 6 5 4 3

To Dr. Wil Baker,
a college friend of my parents,
who now, decades later, has become a wise and
trusted friend to me.
Dr. Baker is an important mentor to Polly as well
and is a huge influence in the life of our family.

Prologue

My name is Andy Andrews. I am a daddy and a husband. I am a friend to some—a good and loyal one, I like to think—and a member of a small community on the Gulf Coast that boasts a population of around four thousand when the tourists aren't using the beach.

I am also a writer and a speaker. As one who communicates as a profession, it is strangely uncomfortable to involve myself or incorporate details of my own life in a book or a presentation, but I understand that it is sometimes necessary. Occasionally, as much as I wish it were not so, the truth in full context simply cannot be achieved until all the facts—including the intricacies of how those facts might be perceived now and in the future— are on the table.

As we begin this story, please allow me to admit I have found no other way around that reality. Therefore, as reluctant as I may be to cast myself as a character in this particular story, I have come to this conclusion: without knowing a few specifics about my own fears and struggles, it would be difficult, if not impossible, to fully understand Jones or the inestimable value his life and words hold *for you* right now . . . today.

At this very moment, if you have ever read one of my books or listened to my audio recordings or seen me on stage, you probably feel as though you know me much better than you know the old man about whom this story will be told. Of course, my own human nature prompts me (even now) to simply shut up and allow you to continue thinking whatever nice things you might have decided about the written and spoken words for which I get credit.

Through the years and many hard lessons, I have found that no matter how long it takes or how desperately a person battles or denies, the truth always—*always*—makes itself known. In addition, even those casual statements we commonly call half-truths, white lies, or exaggerations are costly and embarrassing when they come to light.

Therefore, for the record, allow me to begin with this particular truth: whatever *good* things you think of me, I believe a certain man named Jones to be responsible. He is also responsible for the daddy and husband I am still in the process of becoming. He deserves the credit. His is the life and wisdom and truth you should carefully examine with any time or connection that you possess. And now I am honored to be one of those connections . . .

As I mentioned earlier, I am a writer. I am not the best writer around here or even the only writer in town. I'm just one of several. When I am away from Orange Beach and people ask what I do for a living, I usually hesitate to use the word *author*. For some reason I have always thought the phrase "I am an author!" sounds like someone who considers himself a big deal. I don't. And I am not. If you wanted me to prove it, you could ask what kind of books I write. Any person who has written a book should be able to answer that, right? Honestly, I'm not even sure myself.

I am not attempting to sound humble or pull some "aw, shucks" routine in order to lure you into disagreeing with me about myself. Putting a label on the kind of books I write is like lassoing a bumblebee, and I know it. A mental run-through of traditional publishing labels will tell you very quickly that the task will not be easy. Trust me on this: the best minds in the book business have already tried.

The first book I wrote that was read by anyone other than my family and friends was called *The Traveler's Gift*. It was easy to read and interesting—at least that's what folks said. I thought of it as *a story that includes some of life's principles*. It eventually made the *New York Times* Best Sellers List in the Fiction category, but that same week the book made the *Wall Street Journal* Best-Selling Books list in *Non*fiction. Barnes & Noble placed it in their Self-Improvement section. Amazon.com determined it to be Literature, and there it stayed until they finally settled on the two different categories it still occupies today: Inspiration and Spirituality.

Even the stalwart publication *Publisher's Weekly* struggled to define it. Widely read and greatly respected, *Publisher's Weekly* is an international magazine that has been produced four times a month since 1872, and for the first time in a history of more than one hundred years, *Publisher's Weekly* listed and reviewed a single book—*The Traveler's Gift*—in different sections within a week of each other, in October 2002. Religion loved *The Traveler's Gift* and gushed, "Andrews is an author to watch." The review even compared the book favorably to the Christmas classic *It's a Wonderful Life*. On the other hand, the Fiction section greatly disliked the book and gave it a negative review.

Meanwhile, the *New York Times* kept *The Traveler's Gift* on its bestseller list but decided the book was not fiction after all. They placed it in the Business category. To this day, I walk into most bookstores and still need to ask for help finding the Andy Andrews titles. Believe it or not, I was once escorted to my own books . . . in the Travel section.

So how does one define my writing? I honestly have no idea, and it has caused many a dinner conversation to end in stories and laughter. Perhaps that is why I struggle at times to figure out what it is that I am supposed to put on paper. And there begins our story . . .

One

I found him.

I wasn't looking for him, but there he was, real as life. It was only a glimpse at first, but he stopped and turned, almost as if he felt my gaze upon him. The instant we locked eyes, he grinned. And it was like the old man had never left.

But he did leave. He had disappeared several years ago without so much as a good-bye, and like the old man himself, the circumstances of his departure had been odd. Leaving our tiny, coastal community without being seen by a single person was strange enough—small-town folks don't miss much—but tucking a cryptic message inside a beaten-up suitcase and abandoning it in the middle of a parking lot . . . well, the whole thing had been perplexing. It had also been the number-one topic of conversation in our town for weeks.

In time, however, the residents of Orange Beach came to believe he was gone for good, and a mourning of sorts had settled over the whole community. It wasn't a tragedy. We had suffered through hurricanes and oil spills—we knew what tragedy felt like. It was more of an emptiness we couldn't quite define.

So in lieu of anything specific, we talked endlessly about what we did remember. We discussed his clothes and wondered why we had never seen him in anything other than jeans and a T-shirt. Besides the leather sandals on his feet, that particular ensemble typified his entire wardrobe. We had seen him at a wedding on the lagoon, in restaurants, and even in church a time or two, but never dressed in anything other than jeans and a T-shirt.

No one had ever known where he lived or even where he slept at night. To our knowledge, he had never so much as spent a rainy evening at anyone's house. He didn't own property in our county—we all have friends working at the courthouse, and they checked.

Neither, we all agreed, could he possibly have had a tent in the small brown suitcase that never left his side. And about that suitcase . . . until the day of his disappearance, none of us had ever seen him without it. It was an early weekday morning when Ted Romano, the owner of Pack & Mail, found the old, scuffed-up piece of luggage sitting by itself in the middle of an almost empty parking lot.

Yes, we all had stories about watching the old man struggle through a door with it or carry it with him as he filled a plate from a local salad bar, but as far as we could tell, no one but the man himself had so much as touched that suitcase until the day he vanished.

There was also the age thing. We were almost obsessed with the subject of how old the man might be. We had conceded long before that it was impossible to know his age for sure. His appearance yielded no real clues. "Old" was as close as we could guess. His hair was longish—not long enough for a ponytail, but long*ish*—and as white as polished ivory. Usually only finger-combed, his hair was casually worn and almost beautiful. But his hair was only the first thing about him anyone noticed.

It was the old man's eyes that stopped people in their tracks.

Sparkling as the laughter of a child and imbued with a color I can describe only as tranquil blue, his eyes verged on luminescence. Set against the brown skin of his face and framed by that snowy hair, his eyes would hold a person as long as he cared to talk. And he could really talk . . .

None of us had ever had the opportunity to listen—truly listen—to anyone like him before. It wasn't that he talked a lot. He didn't. It's just that when he *did* talk, the words that tumbled from his mouth were so precise and significant that folks drank in every one.

You may think I am exaggerating, but there are more than a few of us in Orange Beach who credit this old man with changing our lives. In fact, I might be at the top of that long list. But then, my relationship with Jones has spanned more years than anyone else's.

He found me at a particularly tough time in my life when I was twenty-three years old. For several months he was a friend when I didn't have one and told me the truth at a time when I didn't want to hear it. Then he disappeared for close to thirty years.

The next time I saw him was a few years ago when he arrived, as he had the first time, seemingly out of the blue. One awfully curious thing I became aware of during that time was that the old man had apparently been in and out of our town for years. Maybe for decades.

Remember how I said we didn't know how old he was? Well, I talked to some people who were pretty old themselves, and they said the old man had been around when *they* were kids. And they swore up and down that he had been an old man then. Of course, that doesn't make sense to me even now. When I first heard it—and I heard it a lot—I ignored all the talk. Still, I had to admit that he didn't look much different from the first time I had seen him.

His age wasn't the only strange thing about the old man. His skin color was another. He was deeply tanned. Or dark brown. No one could agree on whether his pigmentation had been determined by genetics or a lifelong aversion to sunscreen. As for me, I simply didn't care.

It was curious, however, that African Americans seemed to take it for granted that the old man was black, and Caucasians assumed he was white. I saw it happen so often that I thought it was funny. I even asked him about it once. His answer didn't have much to do with the question, though, and I was not surprised.

I loved the old man, and I was not the only one. And I already told you how much of a difference he made for many of us. But I would be remiss if I did not submit this for consideration as well: there were people in our town who thought the old man was crazy.

It was all very strange . . . how he was mocked and ridiculed by some and the way he just grinned and took it. Some folks— right to his face—even called him names.

Me? I just called him Jones. Not Mr. Jones. Just Jones.

Two

It was a cold night on the Gulf Coast, and I was wearing everything I owned, including an insulated denim jacket I had found in someone's trash. It was almost midnight, and I was coming from a marathon session of cleaning fish for Jeannie's Seafood at the intersection of Highway 59 and the beach road. I was headed back to the Gulf State Park Pier, exhausted and cold, eager to climb under its shelter and sleep.

As was my habit, I got off the main road and walked behind the homes and businesses on the beach. I did this in order to avoid attention from anyone who might wonder what a kid was doing walking the streets of a small beach town alone at night. I was trudging through the concrete pilings under the Pink Pony Pub when Jones joined me.

It was not a surprise, really. I was becoming accustomed to the uncommon way he would commonly appear. This night he simply matched my stride and walked with me. As usual, the old man was in jeans and a T-shirt. "How do you keep from freezing?" I asked.

"I think warm thoughts," Jones replied, before noting, "Woowee! You smell like fish."

Continuing to trudge through the sand with my head down and my hands in my pockets, I said, "Yeah, well, spend a day up to your elbows in twenty-six hundred pounds of 'em, and we'll see what *you* smell like."

Jones was quiet for a while. I suspected he had sensed my mood and was being careful. My current station in life had taken an emotional toll that was not beyond repair. The circumstances were evident, however, even to those who knew me in passing. Jones was aware that I was a threat to fly into a rage or burst into tears or rip someone to pieces with my words. One or more of these crazy manifestations of how I felt at the moment happened far too frequently, and sometimes they happened in public. I didn't want to behave or conduct myself in that manner, but I believed it was nothing I could control. *What can I do?* I often thought. *This is me. This is how I feel. This is just the way I am . . .*

I cut my eyes toward the old man and kept walking. He had a habit of turning up most often, it seemed, when I was tired or depressed or angry. I'd look up from washing someone's boat or pause to stretch while cleaning fish, and there he'd be, over to the side, twenty or thirty feet away, just watching me. He'd smile when I caught him like that, and I didn't mind. After all, he was the only person remotely interested in a young man who was homeless and living on the beach.

The old man could make me laugh, and he did so quite often; but mostly, he made me think. Not necessarily *about* a certain thing . . . He made me think in *ways* I had never considered. Jones had a knack for turning a situation or a deep-seated belief upside down or sideways in such a manner that it became perfectly clear and made total sense.

I didn't look at him again, but I could hear the fine, sugary sand squeaking under his steps. He was quiet, simply offering his company to a lonely young man, and I couldn't help feeling guilty for how I sometimes acted toward him. I often grew frustrated with the old man, sometimes to the point of anger, and then would regret the sharp words I used as I took that frustration out on my friend. In saner moments I wondered if the overwhelming frustration I felt might actually be with myself. I certainly struggled to think the way he did.

"You can't just come up with some answer to everything," I'd said to him only a few nights before. In an ugly tone of voice, I had sneered, "You act like an answer is waiting around the corner, and when you find it—*boom!*—the problem's solved, like somebody waved a magic wand!" I remember stepping close to him for my big finish. With contempt dripping from my words, I had said, "Things are not that simple."

Jones had shrugged and, with the barest hint of a smile, replied, "Seems to me that when the answer appears, the problem *is* solved. You might be scared or frustrated or discouraged or all three, but when you find an answer, life is never the same again. So actually, son . . . things aren't that complicated."

I had wanted to scream.

Approaching the Holiday Inn, we could see that high tide was sending its waves to break upon the foundation of the resort's pool area. Only a seawall protected the hotel's elaborate concrete beach from the waves of the real thing; therefore, it was the only place on our walk where we couldn't stay on the sand. I experienced this obstacle regularly and knew that to avoid wading through the surf, it was necessary to cross the pool deck. Together in the dark, all alone, Jones and I climbed the steps that would allow us to negotiate the array of lounge chairs, circle the pool, and exit the property by way of the stairs on the other side.

Despite the security guard who roamed the hotel grounds at night, I wasn't too scared. The lady who worked the night desk inside the lobby was a middle-aged, African American woman named Beverly. She was also a friend of mine. I called her Mrs. Beverly and occasionally gave her fresh fish as my part of an unspoken agreement that prompted her to look the other way when I used one or another of the hotel's amenities. Still, I was cautious. I didn't want anyone in trouble with the hotel manager. Especially me.

I crouched low, making my way across the deck. Arriving at midpoint, right beside the deep end of the pool, I turned to tell Jones to do the same. I flushed with annoyance, seeing he was *not* bent over and *not* hurrying. The old man was moving casually, absolutely upright, hands in his pockets, with those leather sandals scuffling along the sandy concrete. Having trained myself to avoid attention and the subsequent problems that came with it, I was striving for silence, and the old man's sandals resonated like a metal rake dragging through gravel.

Irritated, I hissed at him to hurry up, get down, and be quiet. But before I could continue my short trek, Jones inexplicably smiled sweetly and reached toward me in a gesture that indicated he wanted to place his hand on my shoulder but instead . . . firmly pushed me into what was a very cold, unheated pool.

I was under the water—all the way under the water—before I had any comprehension of what had just occurred. Years later I would carry a weird mental picture of the old man at that particular instant. I would see him through the surface of the pool, leaning over me with his white hair blowing in the cold wind. As I surfaced with a gasp, Jones was smiling. Not laughing (I might have killed him) but smiling as if he were curious or expectant or fascinated with the object in front of him—which was, of course, me.

I kicked to the side of the pool and grabbed hold of the edge at his feet. All the fire or meanness or whatever it was I carried around was suddenly gone. I wiped my eyes with my hands, looked up at him, and asked, "What was that for?" as he reached down to help me out.

Soon I was wrapped in ten or twelve towels from the Holiday Inn laundry room and drinking coffee from the pot in the lobby. We were sitting on the floor, huddled in the not-quite-inside, not-quite-outside doorway that led to the hotel tennis courts. It was not comfortable, but it was out of the wind, and I was relatively sure we would not be run off.

After giving him the silent treatment for a time—conduct that I must admit had no effect at all—I peered at him sideways and said, "Jones. Man, I don't get you. What in the heck was *that* for?"

He looked up at the ceiling, took a deep, contented breath, and crossed his arms comfortably. "Well," he began, glancing at me briefly, then back to the ceiling. "Son, you are at this very moment in the biggest war you will ever wage in your life. It is confusing, but you're fighting for what you'll one day become. There are forces clashing for space in your head that you don't recognize, can't see, and won't understand until you're able to look back on the whole thing years from now.

"You know, a lot of folks will tell you that little things don't matter." He flashed me a quick look and added, "You'd better turn that on its ear, son. Little things *do* matter. Sometimes, little things matter the most. Everybody pays a lot of attention to big things, but nobody seems to understand that big things are almost always made up of little things. When you ignore little things, they often turn into big things that have become a lot harder to handle.

"'Don't sweat the small stuff,'" Jones said with disdain. "That's a lie that'll ruin your life." He looked hard at me again and locked my gaze with his own. "Your choices, your words, and every move you make are permanent. Life is lived in indelible ink, boy. Wake up. You're making little bitty brushstrokes every minute you walk around on this earth. And with those tiny brushstrokes, you are creating the painting that your life will ultimately become—a masterpiece or a disaster."

Jones shifted in the small space to gain a little comfort and faced me directly when he spoke again. "Okay, back to your question . . ." The old man tilted his head to the side a tiny bit.

"It occurred to me that I wasn't always going to be around to help you with your thinking. So I decided, then and there, that you needed to understand a very important fact about your earthly existence. It is this: Every single day for the rest of your life, somebody is going to push you in the pool. And you'd better decide *now* how you're going to act when it happens."

Jones squinted and leaned toward me. "Are you gonna come out of the water whining? Maybe crying or complaining? Will you come up mad and defiant, threatening everybody? Will you throw fists or worse?

"Or will you come out of the water with a smile on your face? Looking to see what you can learn . . . who you might help? Will you *act* happy though you feel uncertain?"

He stared at me for a beat or two before lowering his chin and speaking in an earnest tone. "It's time to decide, son," he said. "Almost every result that your life produces from this moment forward—good or bad—will depend upon how you choose. Every day, in one form or another, whether you like it or not, you *will* be pushed in the pool. You might as well decide right now how you'll act when it happens."

With that said, Jones got to his feet and left.

I was worn out, tired beyond measure, and I knew I had to leave soon. Before facing the cold night again, however, I dozed, resting somewhat, allowing my mind to drift over and around Jones. I thought again about why he never wore a coat. I thought about where he would sleep that night and about how generally strange he seemed to be. I thought about my life. I thought about Jones's baffling words. And I wondered what in the world I was supposed to make of both.

Three

Present day

The village of Fairhope, Alabama, was founded in November 1894, and for every moment since that time, the salty air has mingled with discarded oyster shells and filtered through the boughs of oak and pine with the occasional trace of fried seafood to create a fragrance unmatched by any lesser town. Tourists come here from all over the world for its shopping, great restaurants, incredible views, and, of course, to stay at the Grand Hotel, recognized as one of the finest golf and sailing destinations in the country.

It was early afternoon on a Monday, and I had driven the forty-five minutes from my home in Orange Beach to Fairhope and was parked in front of the Page & Palette bookstore on Section Street. Shaking my head to clear it, I looked at my watch. How long had I been sitting here? My latest manuscript was overdue, and what I had written, well . . . let's just say that I was not satisfied. In addition to the uncertainty I was inflicting on my publisher, I was at odds with myself and a bit down in the dumps on top of it all.

The root of the problem, I knew, was the type of book every-one expected me to write. For the thousandth time I whined to myself, *If they just wanted a story, I could write a great story. If they wanted just the principles, I could write a straightforward nonfiction book.* Unfortunately the realities of today's modern marketing machine and my own desire to please everyone had combined to yield a fairly strong brand that declared, "Andy Andrews writes stories with principles." Bottom line: I felt trapped. Why? Simply for the reason that *this* time, I had no story.

Oh, I was excited about the principles I had discovered and wanted to teach. In fact, the principles were so powerful that I had already begun to reveal them to the leaders of certain teams and corporations with whom I had long-term contracts. Those cli-ents were already seeing amazing results with the implementation of the new information, but regarding the upcoming book—my typical method for getting the principles into everyone's hands—I didn't have a story. Or, at least, I didn't have *the* story.

In previous books I had always used exciting plotlines as a device to keep the reader's interest as the principle, deftly inserted, made itself known during the action. In *The Heart Mender* I used the true tales of Nazi submarines prowling America's Gulf of Mexico during World War II. An archaeologist and a newspaper reporter chased the origin of a mysteriously powerful object in *The Lost Choice*. I was shaken by the realization that every book I had ever written had a unique and engaging story—something this latest attempt was lacking. I knew it, and with every key-stroke of my Mac, I felt a dangerous hole growing larger beneath me. It was a pit being dug by a shovel of my own creation and fueled by disappointment in myself. Worse, the deeper I dug, the more evidence I found that there was something else in the hole. It was, I recognized, the rising tide of panic.

I looked at my watch again and knew I had to make myself

leave the relative safety of my car. I had promised to drop by Page & Palette and sign their stock of my books. In order to do that, I had to go inside. I love Karin and Keifer, the owners, but I knew that immediately after hugs and hellos would come questions about my next book. "When is it being released?" they would ask. "What is it about? What is the title?" How could I possibly answer their questions? *Oh, I don't know*, I imagined saying, *but my publisher is thrilled with what I have written so far! In fact, just yesterday he called to inform me that I had set a new record for one of their authors. Yes, a new record! Well, no . . . apparently they've never before had anyone under contract miss three separate deadlines on one book. Ah . . . no, sorry I don't have a title for the book. Nope, I haven't figured out the ending either. Actually, I don't know what the book is about. It's all part of a new writing technique: I am keeping everything a big secret. Yes, even from myself . . .*

Without question, I was battling a bit of depression or anxiety or fear . . . or whatever it is that makes me want to sit in my car and never get out. But I *knew* better than to surrender my will. Jones had taught me long before never to give in to a feeling of despair, fear, or defeat. "*Lead* your negative emotions, son," he'd say. "Never allow those emotions to lead you. Always lead them by quickly moving in the opposite direction those emotions insist you should go!" Therefore, knowing full well that I did not even remotely *feel* like it, I smiled—just as the old man had trained me to do. I even chuckled a bit as I opened the car door and stepped out.

Locking the vehicle, I heard a familiar voice. "*Looove* to hear that laughter," the voice boomed. "No sir, we don't allow droopy feelings to put a leash on us!"

I looked up—and there he was. I almost have to repeat it, even in print. There he was, looking like I had just seen him yesterday. What had it been . . . more than five years since he had disappeared? But in a deeper sense it also seemed to be the most natural thing in the world to see that old man. Still, my jaw must have dropped a foot. "Jones?" I managed to croak.

He grinned broadly, held out a small white sack, and as if he saw me every day at this time, said, "Hello, young man. Have a lemon bar?"

I was too stunned by his sudden appearance to answer coherently, so I simply laughed as I alternately shook his hand and tried to hug him. Then I babbled like a four-year-old with his first glazed doughnut while the old man who had meant so much to me smiled and waited patiently for me to calm down.

Finally, at a loss for words, I realized that I was still holding fast to Jones's right arm, the one that held the little white bag. "You don't have to mug me for it," he said laughingly, gently prying my fingers from his bicep. "I have an extra one."

"One what?" I managed, my mind moving in several directions at once.

"An extra lemon bar," he answered calmly. "I got two. There's one for each of us." He paused for a moment before waving his hand in my face. "Hey, you in there?"

"Yes," I answered. "I mean, yes sir. I am in here." Then I blurted, "Jones, don't leave."

"Settle down, and let's find a place to sit. How 'bout a cup of coffee to go with these treats?" He glanced toward Page & Palette. Quickly, though, he looked away and muttered, "No . . . you don't need any coffee. You're jittery enough."

Steering me down the sidewalk to an empty bench, he gestured for me to sit, and I did. Joining me, the old man opened the sack and produced two lemon bars. The delicate cakes were from Latte Da, the bookstore's coffee shop, as anyone who has ever set foot in the town of Fairhope would know. The quaint emporium is almost as famous for its coffee and pastries as it is for its books, and folks come from far corners of the world to experience the unique atmosphere of this beautiful independent bookstore.

Taking a lemon bar in my right hand, I positioned my left under it to catch any of the powdered sugar that might otherwise fall and be wasted. As I put it to my mouth, a peculiar thought wiggled its way into my head. So before taking a bite, I turned instead to the old man, who, I noted, already had an innocent look on his face before I said a word.

Plunging ahead anyway, I smiled and offered my question. "Jones . . . did you buy two lemon bars for yourself? I think you were expecting someone. In fact, I think that—"

"Let's be careful," Jones said, interrupting me and patting me on the knee, "that we don't read too much into a trivial occurrence."

The smile remained, but my eyes narrowed. "Jones, there has never been anything trivial about you, and you know it." He shrugged as if he did not know *what* I was talking about, but I knew that he did. And *he* knew that I knew. I had spent too much time with the old man to believe anything that ever happened around him was coincidence.

"Can I ask why you're here? Here in Fairhope, I mean. And why did you leave Orange Beach? Jones, it's been five years since anyone has heard from you. Where have you been? Also, where are you staying? Can I help you with anything? Will you at least come home with me to spend a couple of nights? Polly and the boys would love to see you. What are you doing in Fairhope anyway?"

"You're jabbering again," Jones said patiently as he took the last bite of his lemon bar. Wiping the sugar from his hand onto his jeans, he added, "And you asked the Fairhope question twice. You know, you sure do talk a lot. I'm thinking you'd get more books written if you could curb that tendency. Hard to write and talk at the same time. At least that's what I suspect."

At that mild rebuke I fell silent and looked away from him. "Oh, come on," Jones said as he poked at me with his elbow. "I seen little kids who could pout better'n that." He gave me half a moment to put a grin back on my face, then asked, "You gonna talk or what?"

I turned toward him and said simply, "I have really missed you." With that pronouncement, he put his arm around my shoulder again, and for some reason I almost burst into tears.

I don't mind admitting that, at that moment, I was uncharacteristically an emotional wreck. For some reason I had always felt like a child around Jones. Not childish, but somehow child-*like*. That day, I asked him, "Did you miss me too?" just like a kid would have.

Of course, he responded in his typical manner. "Nope," Jones said. "To miss you, I'da had to been gone. And I ain't been gone. I've been around."

I knew better than to question that answer. Instead, I made some comment about his reply being typical of him, and it was exactly that. Jones had always been a walking contradiction. He was the only person I had ever met who could be aggravating, encouraging, evasive, straightforward, demanding, and comforting all at the same time. I wanted to ask him *why* he was in Fairhope, but I knew his answer would have been something like, "Why not?" so I didn't even bother.

I did, however, question him about how long he had been in town. Again, his reply left me shaking my head. "Not really certain how long I been here," Jones stated as a matter of fact. "That doesn't really matter to me, so I choose not to think about it. But I've been here more'n a couple of days, that's for sure."

After a brief pause he wrinkled up his face as if he were giving the thought every ounce of his concentration and said, "Time is an odd thing. Christmas Eve for most adults lasts about as long as most other nights, but for an eight-year-old, on that particular night of the year, time slows to a crawl." Jones laughed and slapped his hands together. "And I don't know if you ever thought about it," he said, "but what you and I calculate in years, in reality, might be just a quick dusting of heavenly hands.

"Think about it like this," he said, shifting on the bench to face me. "What are you planning for next year . . . on today's date?"

I laughed. "I have no clue. Are you kidding?"

"No," he said. "I'm not kidding. A year from now seems like a long way off, though, doesn't it?"

"A year from now?" I replied. "Yes. A year from now is forever. I mean, I'm not even thinking about next *month*."

Jones nodded. "How old are your boys now? Eleven and fourteen, aren't they?" I confirmed their ages, and he continued.

"A year or a month or even a week into the future can seem like a long time away. But a decade in the past?" He snapped his fingers. "Why, don't it seem like those boys were born just a minute ago?"

The old man seemed to have run out of steam. With a satisfied sigh Jones eased back down on the bench beside me and placed one leg over the other. "Yes sir," he said softly. "Time is an odd thing. Currency is what it is. Once spent . . . it's gone forever." And with that he simply crossed his arms and closed his eyes.

I wasn't sure if he was resting or waiting for me to talk. He was quiet and appeared relaxed, and I didn't know what to say, so I didn't say anything at all.

As I studied the profile of his familiar face, I couldn't help but reflect upon where I might have ended up had it not been for that old man and the "time" he had spent with me. After all, I was living under a pier when he found me. But now . . . ? I considered what was, in fact, the relatively small amount of time

I had been in his presence and tried to pinpoint what he had done—I mean, *exactly* what he had done—that had made such a dramatic difference in my life.

It was my *thinking*, I decided. Jones had challenged the very foundations of my thought processes. He questioned my perceptions, my assumptions, and even—or maybe I should say *especially*—my conclusions. Yes, I nodded to myself. That is exactly how he had managed to change my life so many years ago.

Within thirty minutes of our meeting for the first time, Jones had asked, "Do you read?" His question seemed simple enough, but as it turned out, there was a lifetime of layers to the true answer—an answer that continues to unfold even now, after all these years. When he had asked, "Do you read?" I remember taking a breath to answer affirmatively as he had added, "I'm not asking if you *can* read; I'm asking if you *do*."

And that was only the first time Jones challenged what I thought I knew or even what I thought I had heard. The shift he created in my thinking at that moment changed my answer to his question from a yes to a no.

"Proper perspective about every facet of your existence," he would tell me again and again, "is only everything."

And so, as Jones became a fixture in my broken life—remember, I was homeless at the time—his remarkable way of dissecting situations began to have an astounding effect on me. And the books didn't hurt either.

"Jones? Are you asleep?" I said softly. He made no response, so I sat back and waited. For the moment, I was content to simply sit there, feeling an odd sense of importance, as if I were protecting him somehow.

After all, I wasn't the same scared kid he had found living on the beach years ago. Things had changed for me during the three-plus decades that had followed. Professionally—except for the hiccup with my latest manuscript—I was doing fairly well, and my personal life was on a great track. I had married a beautiful woman with whom I was still madly in love, and together we were in the process of raising our two boys.

I smiled, watching as the old man's breathing gently lifted his brown arms, which remained folded across his midsection. "Come here, son," was what he had said to me that night—the first time I had ever seen him—so long ago. Then he had reached out his hand and added, "Move into the light." And that is exactly what I have been trying to do ever since.

Not a day has gone by in more than thirty years that I haven't thought of Jones. More specifically, I don't believe a day has passed since that time when I haven't rolled those particular four words around in my head: *move into the light*.

At first, as you might expect, I assumed it had been the pier light to which he was referring. When I lived under the pier and night fell, my only light came from the big sodium-vapor bulb that extended from the top of a pole high above the structure. A small slice of that light worked its way down to me through a crack between the huge slabs of concrete. Those massive blocks of cement were set end to end and formed the pier's walkway. They also served as the ceiling to my secret—and very sandy—home.

In the weeks after my first encounter with the old man, it began to dawn on me that the light to which he had been referring was a much brighter source of illumination than I had originally assumed. And the way things turned out, that light— and its source—changed everything.

"It's six minutes after two o'clock," Jones said. He had not moved a muscle. His arms were still crossed. His right leg draped across his left, and his eyes were still closed. I glanced at my phone. He was correct. It was exactly 2:06. Jones had never worn a watch, but I smiled to myself as I looked at his wrists to check anyway. Surveying the area with a few turns of my head, I also determined there were no clocks within sight at which he could have taken a quick peek.

I had seen the old man do this many times, and it always amazed me. He never missed. I mean, he *never, ever* missed by even a minute. Taking a deep breath, I opened my mouth to ask for at least the millionth time just how he managed that trick, but before I could utter a word, Jones added, "You're supposed to pick up the boys from school. From here to there is at least fifty minutes with no traffic. You'd better get going and hightail it."

Surprised as always at his awareness, I nodded. "Okay," I replied.

With the barest hint of a smile, Jones said, "Good." Then he shut the one eye he had opened for our brief conversation and settled in with small movements as if he were readying himself for a long nap. Once again, he said, "Good," and with a deep breath in and a long one out, Jones was asleep.

He really was asleep. Or at least I thought so. The old man could read people and situations like no one I had ever seen or even heard of. Sometimes, during his long absences from my life, I imagined Jones watching me through a pane of glass. I would wonder what he would think about this situation or that person.

Then after five years, or thirty years, of being wherever else he went, Jones would show up and act as though we had seen each other an hour ago. It was weird. And wonderful. There was so much I wanted to know about him, but he was never interested in anything more than my life and what I was learning about myself.

I looked at the time again and knew I had to leave. I seriously considered shaking him and waking him up. I wanted to know where he would be and how I might find him. Was he staying in town? With someone? Inside? Outside? As much as I loved Jones, this part of our relationship was infuriating. As to where I might see him again . . . or *when* I might see him again . . . I had no clue.

But then I got one.

Out of time but still needing to sign books, I reluctantly turned away and quickly moved toward Page & Palette's front door. Casually aware of the vivid colors of the posters and book covers splashed across the store window, I froze as my hand touched the doorknob. There, in the far bottom left corner of the glass storefront, was a small, hand-lettered sign. In reality a 3x5 index card, the sign was ridiculously overwhelmed by the colors and commercial designs of the larger, more expensive advertisements competing for attention.

I moved to the unassuming, handwritten notice and went to one knee to get a closer look. At the top of the card, the words PARENTING CLASS had been neatly printed in all caps in blue ink with a ballpoint pen. THURSDAY AT 7 PM AND SAME TIME NEXT THURSDAY FOR SURE was centered on the next line. Under that, in parentheses, was written (AFTER THAT, WE'LL SEE HOW IT GOES). The location, GRAND HOTEL, was listed on the last line—and there, at the bottom, in careful script, was the signature of the teacher: *Jones*.

My mouth opened slightly as my eyebrows reached for the top of my head. I was past the point of believing that anything Jones said or did could surprise me anymore, but this . . . well, this was a surprise. I didn't know what to think. Looking back to my old friend, I saw that he hadn't moved. He remained upright on the park bench, arms crossed, chin on his chest. Yes, Jones was still asleep, but my mind raced with the possibilities of how this newest little wrinkle might play out.

Before heading inside the bookstore, I glanced at him one more time. Then with a huge grin on my face, I pushed the door open, shaking my head in amazement, and laughed out loud.

At least I knew where to find him. And when.

Four

The old man stopped for a moment to push his hair out of his eyes and brush a few strands of pine straw from his clothes. He had already walked a long way and was slipping quietly through the woods. It was almost an hour before sunrise, but Jones could see well in the dark. The raccoons and deer and armadillos—even one bobcat—paid little attention to him as he drifted through their midst.

The old man loved this part of the day. He didn't need much sleep and preferred to be alone during the early morning hours. Oftentimes, though, he took on a project that required his work to begin in the dark. In a way, Jones knew, *every* journey started in the dark. And that, of course, was the very essence of his reason for being. It was his purpose. Jones took folks by the hand and helped them see the pathway by which they could move into the light. Perspective, he called it.

Jones walked across several cultivated fields, careful not to damage the growing crops. He could hear the noise ahead. From where he stopped to listen, it sounded like a muffled version of scratchy audio from an infinite number of speakers. He was still more than a mile from its source.

The noise grew louder as he walked until, at last, he stopped inside the woods at the edge of a huge field. Jones could see the faintest hint of light beginning to appear in the eastern sky. Alone in the darkness, he grinned at the clamoring racket now building to a crescendo around him.

After a time, cautiously, as if in slow motion, the old man moved into the middle of the field. It was no longer pitch black. The bluish-gray shadows portended the coming dawn while the tumult was growing. The very air popped and whistled and creaked. Metallic clacking and distinctive rattles filled the retreating darkness as if to scare it away forever. Screams of anger kept company with caustic rolling purrs and repeated shrieks of delight.

As night was gradually overtaken by the morning's initial glow, the uproar increased, intensifying in volume, enthusiastically anticipating the split second when the sun's earliest ray would vault over the horizon. Jones stood motionless in the field's center. Head bowed, eyes closed, he was perfectly still for several full minutes when—as expected, but without notice—the sun's first beam burst across the field. The old man's white hair shimmered as the light fluoresced everything in its path. And for a beat . . . two at the most . . . everything went silent.

At that moment the noise responded to the dawn, more piercing than before, followed immediately by swirling images, coalescing across the morning sky into one shape-shifting symphony of motion. Jones looked up and smiled.

It was pandemonium.

It had been full daylight for at least twenty minutes. Baker Larson, alone in his Ford F-150, leaned forward and scanned the sky through a dirty windshield. Slowing the red truck slightly, he spotted the object of his search several miles away. The young farmer never took his eyes off the point in the distance as he tossed a curse word into the stale air of the pickup and punched the accelerator. Without any conscious thought, Baker snatched up the plastic cup in the drink holder and put it to his chin, spitting into it a stream of tobacco juice that was as foul as his mood.

County Road 33 was long and straight. Fortunately for everyone else this morning, the two-lane blacktop was clear because the driver's mind was far away, and the Ford was being pushed well beyond the speed limit.

Baker Larson had turned thirty-seven years old the day before. It had been a Monday he would never forget. The bank sent a registered letter in which the word *foreclosure* was mentioned prominently in several paragraphs. "Happy birthday to me," Baker had said aloud after reading it.

Obviously there had not been much of a celebration. Sealy, his wife, had already purchased thick rib eyes for the grill as a surprise, but Baker was upset about the cost of the steaks; therefore, any party atmosphere that might have been possible was over before the evening started.

Their daughters were high school age and already working to help the family make ends meet. For once, Sealy had been glad the girls worked evenings—thank God for waitressing jobs. At least they weren't there to experience their father's grumpy behavior on what was supposed to have been a joyful occasion.

Baker and Sealy had married young and struggled financially from the start. There had been no inheritance from either side of the family, and both carried student loans from two years of community college.

Sealy had gone to college because everyone else did, and she had never really decided what she wanted to do. She knew she wanted Baker, and she knew she wanted children. After eighteen years together, by most standards, the couple had a successful marriage. But the stress never really went away.

In retrospect, Baker was glad he had gone to college because that was where he met Sealy, but he had not known what he wanted to do either. It was a fact he recalled every month when the payment was made on his student loan. He had earned a two-year degree, but he did not want any part of any job for which that particular degree qualified him. It had never occurred to him to determine in advance just what kind of job he could obtain with that degree. Apparently it had never occurred to his faculty advisors, either, because no one ever mentioned it to him. Baker often wondered if his guidance counselors were still paying off their student loans too.

When sixty acres of land became available between Fairhope and Foley, Baker jumped on it. He had worked on some of the Baldwin County farms during his summers in high school and figured he could own one as easily as work on someone else's. He wasn't too surprised that he qualified for the loan—it was a government thing—but he was shocked that they offered him more than he needed to buy the place. The extra money, he was told, was for seed, fertilizer, and anything else he might need.

The first thing Baker had "needed" was a new truck. A brandnew truck. And a new one for Sealy. Baker was determined to have the best of everything on his farm, and, for the most part, by borrowing available cash, that was one particular goal he managed to accomplish.

He used the money from government loan programs and farm subsidies for hunting vehicles and elaborate playhouses for the girls. Five years after they were married, Baker and Sealy acquired a four-bedroom, three-bath residence in town. Of course, the house was mortgaged to the hilt (just like everything else they had), and through the years it became increasingly obvious that the family's finances left no margin for unexpected occurrences.

Baker had juggled things for a long time, but the letter from the bank let him know with certainty that the balls were no longer in the air. He felt scared, embarrassed, angry, confused, weak, and tired. Oh, and stupid. Especially stupid.

And guilty. Guilty because of the damage he had done to his family's future. Baker had told his wife and daughters that they were going to be rich. He certainly believed it. Money was all Baker ever thought about, really, and the arrogance he displayed with the things he bought—never mind that it was all on credit—bordered on the ridiculous. Somewhere in his subconscious Baker knew that his lust for stuff was some kind of reaction to a family history about which he was ashamed. His daddy had died broke after four marriages, and though no one ever, ever talked about it, Baker knew that his grandfather had died in prison.

The extended family was just as bad. Most of the young farmer's cousins and their kids were always in trouble of one sort or another. He had an aunt who was constantly in either rehab or the county jail. Then there was his uncle Edward, the preacher, who was always broke, and the church paid for his house. It disgusted Baker that "Brother Ed" always lectured them about God providing but never hesitated to ask his nephew for money, never called it a loan, and never bothered to pay any of it back. Ever!

His mother's side was no better. Her own brother had not come to her funeral but *had* managed to make it to the house several hours after it was over. He used the same flat-tire excuse they had heard at least a dozen times. He wanted to pick up some things, he said, "to remember her by." Less than a week later Sealy spotted those things remembering Baker's mama in a pawnshop window.

Yes, Baker's family tree was a mess, especially when it came to their finances. On the other hand, when he looked around at most everyone else, he couldn't help but come to the conclusion that debt and financial stress were just part of success. So while he did not like the pressure, he did consider it normal. In the back of his mind, though, the farmer felt like he was running on the edge of a cliff. The expenses and the income had balanced pretty closely for years, but he always lived in fear about the one thing that kept the banks at bay. His crops.

A full harvest was the only way he paid the note. A farmer could only hope that his crops were successful enough to allow him to do it all again the following year. "How'd you like to throw all your money on the ground," went the old saying, "and hope there was enough left to pick up several months later so you could throw it all on the ground again?"

Yeah, Baker often thought, *farmers feed the world. We also keep the antacid companies in business.*

It was a quandary unique to agriculture. Would there be too much water or not enough water? Is this too much pesticide? Too much fertilizer? Or not enough of either? Too much sun? Is all this wind dry-burning the leaves? There's not enough wind for pollination. Planting too early? Too late? Unfortunately for farmers, the cliché really was true: hindsight is 20/20. The second-guessing never stopped.

Last June had been the first time Baker missed a payment. It seemed as though the rain, which had been needed so desperately months before, would never stop falling during the spring. Severe thunderstorms had washed out the rows of seed corn almost immediately after planting. The kernels that did sprout came up in clumps that were finally reduced to decomposing mush by the weeks of rain that followed.

That month Baker had skipped payments on the land

and the house, using the money instead to replant the field in September. The collards and broccoli got a good start, and Baker was optimistic that he would right their financial ship with the harvest in November, but when October rolled in and out without any rain at all, he knew he was in trouble.

For a time it seemed as if it just might work out. Baker and Sealy had talked to their creditors about a last-ditch effort with wheat; and while no one was happy, they all knew there was no other alternative but to try. It rained just the right amount throughout the early months of the new year, and when the weather warmed significantly, the wheat was a sight to behold, growing taller and thicker by the day. Baker and Sealy often drove slowly around the edge of the field and watched and laughed as the winds blew swirling patterns in the long grass.

Their great spirits lasted until several weeks before the projected harvest when Baker noticed a few browning plants. He had never planted wheat but had followed common practices and used tips he gleaned from local farmers or found online. He had been closely monitoring the moisture content, and it had always been within the parameters set for his area. *Maybe*, he thought, *this is just a small section of the field that received less rain*. But no, within a week the brown, shriveling plants were everywhere.

It was the Hessian fly, Baker was informed, one of wheat's most devastating pests the world over. His field was calculated by the county farm agent to be at a level of 58 percent infestation. Of course, that meant a total loss. There was no combine harvester that could reap a field and target only the wheat stalks that were not affected.

For more than a week after the traumatic pronouncement about his field, Baker had kept alive the crazy idea that maybe he and his family might harvest the good wheat by hand and at least be able to stave off their creditors. Then, three days ago, the starlings had showed up.

It was absolutely unbelievable. Baker had never been particularly religious—and the past year had certainly not nudged him in that direction—but it was simply inconceivable to him that multiple disasters of this magnitude could befall him by chance. First too much rain, followed by not enough rain. Then, at last, when the rain actually fell in the perfect amount, bugs ruined half the crop and birds ate the rest. It was a plague, Baker decided, of biblical proportions.

On this particular morning Baker's wasn't the only location being targeted by the starlings. Other farmers in the area were taking hits, too, but at the moment, Baker only cared about his field. The birds were here by the millions. The vast flocks, he was told, had not invaded Baldwin County for years. Yet here they were, just for him it seemed, during the one year that really mattered.

Baker Larson was about to lose everything. He was out of moves, inconsolable, empty of hope, and full of rage. And he had a gun.

Arriving at the southeast corner of his field, Baker slowed the truck briefly and looked at the sky filled with birds before slamming the gearshift into low and plowing on through the broad ditch in front of him. There were four entrances to the sixty-acre plot that the farmer could have used, but he was so enraged at the sight of the winged destruction and the thought of his ruined life that he simply didn't take the time. He drove right out into the doomed wheat, spinning his tires and cursing, toward the largest concentration of starlings.

Moments later, still a couple of hundred yards away from the birds, Baker skidded to a stop and stared. His eyes had been on the flocks wheeling through the air, but there was someone in the field under them. It was a man, Baker decided, an old man and obviously a lunatic. The guy was bending and turning and waving his arms around. First one arm would reach and wave or move, then the other. Then both arms at the same time.

Baker watched only a minute before jerking the gearshift into park. Stepping from the truck, he thought, *I'll put a stop to this*. The birds were flying together, Baker saw, in some odd motion that made the flock look as if it had a mind of its own. And they seemed to stay close to the crazy guy, wheeling above and around him. It appeared as if the old man was enjoying the show and his arm motions were attempting to follow the movement of the flock. Either way, Baker intended to kill a few and get this old man off his land. At least, while it still was his land.

The farmer had shut the door of the truck when he got out and didn't bother to open it back up. He simply reached through the open driver's side window and pulled a shotgun from the rack mounted on the back window. Baker kept the gun's chamber empty, but the magazine was fully loaded. It was a Remington 1187, a 12-gauge, semiautomatic. The plug was out, so when Baker jacked a shell filled with Number Sixes in the chamber and started walking toward the old man, there were still three shells in the magazine.

As the agitated young farmer stalked closer and closer to the old man, he maneuvered around to approach the guy from directly behind. The guy was clearly nuts. Baker knew that for sure now. He was less than a hundred yards away and could hear the man talking or yelling to the birds, which continued to fly in weird, tight groups around him.

Baker Larson didn't know it, but he was witnessing a murmuration. No one knows why they do it, yet, occasionally, hundreds of thousands—sometimes millions—of starlings gather in great shape-shifting flocks called *murmurations*.

After decades of observation researchers continue to be uncertain *how* they do this. The starling murmurations are an example of "swarm intelligence," which is also seen in vast schools of fish. So far, even complex algorithmic models have not been able to explain the starling flock's unique ability for group acrobatics. What has been measured, however, is the reaction time of the individual birds flying as a group. Flying as if controlled by a single brain, the birds use just under one-tenth of a second to move as a team or group and successfully avoid midair collisions.

Baker closed to ten yards. The crazy man was apparently oblivious to his presence, and the starlings were flying so close he wanted to duck. Instead, he raised the gun to his shoulder, punched off the safety with his right forefinger, and pointed it at the middle of the swarm. Baker pulled the trigger three times in quick succession, and stricken birds rained down around the two men while the flock made a panicked escape.

Even as he shot, Baker had kept an eye on the old man, who had both arms in the air when the blasts ripped into the flock. Strangely, the man did not react immediately with the terror Baker was expecting. Instead, he barely moved at all, continuing to hold up his arms for several long seconds as the starlings fled and the gunfire faded away. Only then did he allow his arms to fall to his side and carefully begin to turn around.

The farmer had taken two quick steps after the shots, and when the object of his immediate attention finally turned to face him, Baker was even closer and had the long gun pointed right at the old man's head. His cheek was on the stock, his right eye sighting down the twenty-eight-inch barrel. "Don't you move, old man," he threatened. "I will put you down."

Five

The circle shape that is formed by the end of a 12-gauge can seem larger than it really is if the gun is close. This is especially true when the gun is pointed between one's eyes. The old man had been instructed not to move, and, for the moment, he was more than willing to comply. The farmer holding the gun, on the other hand, was so enraged that he was trembling, a fact that did not escape the old man's attention.

"Who are you?" the farmer demanded. "What're you doing here?" The gun wavered again. Sweat streamed down Baker's forehead and into his eyes, forcing him to wipe his face quickly with his left hand. Firming up his grip on the gun again, he inched even closer. "Did you hear me? I said—"

"Yes, I can hear you," the old man said softly.

Baker yelled, "What? What? Speak up! What's your name?" all the while becoming more menacing in his body language.

"Jones," the old man said. "My name is Jones."

"What're you doing here? This is private property."

"Yes, I know," Jones said. "I am where I'm supposed to be. I actually came to see you. Just got here a little early is all. There's no reason to get upset."

The farmer never took his cheek from the gunstock and said, "You old fossil, you don't know anything about why I might be upset. And there is no reason for you to be here to see me. I'm not hiring. I ought to shoot you for trespassing."

At that, Jones's demeanor changed abruptly. The passive look on his face disappeared. He rolled his eyes as if he had had enough and stepped forward, pushing the barrel of the 12-gauge from his face and taking it from the farmer's hands without a struggle. Pointing the gun away from them in an obvious manner, Jones stepped a few yards to Baker's right. Expertly, it appeared, he put on the safety, ejected the lone shell from the gun's chamber, and caught it in the air.

Returning to Baker with the shotgun still pointed in a safe direction, Jones flung the remaining shell out into the wheat. At that moment, Jones's attention was attracted to something on the ground. He stopped, shifting the gun into his other hand, and reached down. As he did so, Jones's piercing gaze moved upward and into the eyes of the young man in front of him. Without looking away, the old man carefully picked up one of the dead starlings.

The old man looked away from Baker and shifted the shotgun into the crook of his arm. With great care he placed the starling onto his right hand, where its still-bleeding breast pressed down against his palm. The bird was darkly colored but glistening with a shine accented by the speckled pattern that was typical of a starling. Though the bird was a duplicate of millions just like it, the one in the old man's hand was stunning. Even in death, its glossy feathers of blackest black seemed polished by the highlighted flecks of deep green.

Contrasting distinctly with the dark, glimmering feathers was the bird's bright yellow beak. Now relaxed, it was slightly open, displaying the tiny pink tongue it had protected in life. Longer than that of a comparably sized bird, the starling's beak is unique in all the world. Its gentle curve synchronizes perfectly with a razor's sliver of a tongue in order to source the starling's astonishing ability to produce thousands of distinct sounds.

Moving the bird from one hand to the other and turning it over in the process, the old man looked at Baker and said simply, "This was a female."

Good, the young farmer thought. *I'm glad. At least that'll be one less nest of babies to grow up and destroy someone else's life.*

The old man directed his attention back to the bird. Now upturned in his left hand, the starling's head lay to the side. The ruined breast, open and ugly, was now visible, and her wings, capable of speed and acrobatics only moments ago, hung limp and were opened wide.

Baker stood three feet away and didn't know why he didn't just leave, but he remembered the old man still had his gun, so he waited and watched. He had seen something in the old man's face a few seconds before that had made him want to run. *What is up with this guy?* he thought. *What kind of look was that? Mad as a hornet and about to cry at the same time . . . very weird.*

Still, Baker watched. He was more than a bit aggravated on top of everything else. *I'm the one standing here with his life ruined, and this old dude is acting like I shot one of his pets*, Baker raged silently. *Dang, man! Get over it. There're a jillion starlings flying around here, and every single bird is just like the one in your hand.*

The starling's open wings revealed the absence of green speckles on their undersides. They were jet black. The old man eased the bird up to his face as if he were inspecting it as thoroughly as he could. Of course, Baker was so close, the bird was practically in his face as well. Staring, Baker blinked hard two times. His mind was racing. The old man put his fingertip on the starling's feathers and gave a little push. When he pulled his hand back, a white spot was left behind.

Baker blinked again and moved his head so he could see. Yes, there it was, a white spot—a brilliant white—right in the middle of the underside of the starling's right wing. Was it paint? Baker didn't think so and wasn't sure where the old guy would have gotten paint in the first place. Then, weirdest of all, Baker thought, the old man closed the starling's wings and put the bird into his pocket.

He paused only for a moment before moving a few feet away, and in a practiced manner, pulled back the shotgun's breach bolt with his right hand and tilted the chamber to show it was empty. After everything that had preceded it, only then did Jones hand the gun back to the farmer.

Baker stood openmouthed, not quite understanding what had just happened. He hadn't really wanted to shoot this old guy in the first place, but he hadn't walked over here intending to let him have the gun either. But that's what he had done. Then he had stood there, like an idiot, and waited through a bird funeral of some kind for the guy who had taken his gun to give it back!

"Now look here, Baker Larson," Jones said sternly. "I know you're having a bad time of it, but if your foolish thinking is going to have you pointing guns at people, there won't be much I can do." Then he added, "You keep acting *that* ridiculous, there might not be much I *want* to do."

"Hey," Baker said as if he were just waking up, "how did you know my name? Have we met?"

"Of course we've met, son. You think I pulled your name out of the air? Now sit down, Baker."

Curiously, the strong voice Baker obeyed without question reminded him an awful lot of someone from his past. He couldn't place the memory, though, and his brain was scattering in several directions at once.

"What were you doing with those birds when I came up?

And that one bird . . . the one you touched . . ." Baker had put the shotgun aside and watched as the old man settled cross-legged directly in front of him. Noting that Jones had not answered his question, the farmer asked several more. "Is Jones your last name? You're Mr. Jones? Where are you from?"

Jones sighed, and with that rush of breath most of his aggravation with the young man before him seemed to dissipate as well. He reached out his right hand and smiled. "I'm thinking we should start over. Hm? I am Jones. Not Mr. Jones. Just Jones. And at the moment I am from Fairhope."

Baker hesitated only a fraction of a second before reaching out as well. As he shook the older man's hand, he forced a small laugh and said, "Glad I didn't shoot you." He glanced around and added, "Ah . . . what are we doing?"

"You and I are about to have a little talk."

"Oh. Well, hey, you know, it's nice to meet you and all. And I'm sorry about that a few minutes ago, but um . . . I really have a lot to do. So . . ." Baker started to get to his feet. He wasn't sure why he was on the ground in the first place.

"Son," Jones said, "you don't have anything to do."

Baker froze. "What?" he said. He was offended. At the same time his mind was registering the fact that the old man in front of him was correct. He did not have anything to do. "Yes, I do have something to do," he huffed anyway. "I'm—"

"You do *not*"—Jones broke in evenly—"have anything to do." At that, the farmer's shoulders slackened, and he eased back to the ground.

Jones continued as if he had not been interrupted. "You do not have anything to do. Baker Larson, at this moment in your life, there is nowhere else for you to go. You have run as hard and as fast and as long as you can run. Until right now, right here. You have finally cornered yourself in this disaster of a wheat field. You have called yourself a farmer, but you . . . and your father . . . and your father's father . . . have been planting bad seeds for many years."

All the air seemed to go out of Baker at that moment. There was no anger, no aggression. He wanted to cry or die or melt into the ground. "Who are you, man?" he said to Jones. "For real. Why are you here? Why am I here?"

Jones cocked his head and showed a hint of a smile. "Why are you here? Why am I here? Those are questions Socrates and Aristotle asked centuries ago. Is it possible that you and I might find the answer today in Baldwin County?"

Baker returned the old man's smile with a weak one of his own and said, "Yeah, probably not. I really meant . . . ah . . . I guess I meant, why are we together? Did something happen to me? I'm feeling strange. And no offense, but I feel weird sitting out here with you. I think I need to go home."

Jones nodded. "What you are experiencing right now . . . what you are doing, what you are thinking . . . It doesn't seem normal, does it?"

"No," Baker said. "It doesn't."

"Okay . . . good." Jones narrowed his eyes as if he were coming to some great conclusion. Nodding again, he brightened. "I'm sure that's a feeling you can get used to. And, hey, I suppose you'll *have* to get used to it if you want something from life other than what you have right now. Correct?"

Baker frowned. "What's that supposed to mean?"

"It's pretty simple, son," Jones said. "Normal isn't the goal."

"I'm not . . ." Baker shook his head. "What?"

"Normal," Jones said slowly, "is not what you want to be."

Baker still didn't understand. "I don't want to be normal? What? I'm supposed to want to be *abnormal*?"

Jones chuckled. "Well, you don't have to express it in those terms," he said, "but that's the idea." Leaning back on one elbow, he stretched out his legs and said, "Look, Baker, you've been 'normal' your whole life. How's that working out?"

The young farmer didn't say anything, so Jones continued. "You are thirty-seven years old and—"

Baker stiffened. "Hey man, how do you know how old I am?"

"You look thirty-seven," Jones replied. "Who cares? That's not the point. The point is that for a lot of years, you have paid way too much attention to doing things the way everyone around you considers normal. Trying to achieve something great by doing things the normal way is like expecting to win the lottery by purchasing a single ticket and being one of millions of people who have done the same thing. It's not likely to happen."

Baker grunted. "Achieve something great? What are you talking about? I quit thinking I was going to do something great in the eighth or ninth grade."

Jones spread his hands and grinned. "Of course you did. So did most everybody else. In fact, at that age it's an incredibly *normal* thing to do."

Baker cocked his head and gave the old man a sly look. "I'm sitting on the ground in the middle of a sixty-acre field with an old dude I almost shot a few minutes ago . . . That is not normal."

Jones laughed and after hesitating briefly, Baker joined in. "Okay," Jones said, "that's a start."

As quickly as he had laughed a moment before, Baker's demeanor grew grim. "So what's this all got to do with me?" he asked. "And you . . . Seriously, man. I don't know you. What do you do?"

Jones looked at the younger man thoughtfully. "I guess you could say that I'm in the transportation business, son. I help folks get from where they are . . . to where they want to be."

Baker nodded, though he wasn't sure he believed it. He thought the old guy looked more like a bum.

"I'm considering teaching a bit of that philosophy to a few folks around here," Jones said. "Soon, in fact. Sort of an informal class. What do you think?"

"It would be different," the farmer said without enthusiasm.

"You are exactly right," Jones said and reached over to slap Baker on the knee. "Thank you for pointing that out. It would be different. Therefore, the class absolutely must convene." Jones scrambled to his feet and pulled the younger man up with him. "I will be in touch because you need to attend," he said and turned to walk away.

"Hang on," Baker said. "Man, I appreciate the . . . ah . . . encouragement or whatever—you know, all the stuff you just said. But I don't really know you, and . . . I'm just sayin.' I'm busy. I have a lot coming down on me right now, and I don't know about coming to some class."

Jones walked the few steps back to the farmer and stuck out his hand. Baker took it to shake, but the old man did not let go. "Okay, Baker," Jones said. "I totally understand." Not relaxing his grip on the younger man's hand, Jones also held him with his eyes. "I know you don't want to come to a class or listen to a—what did you call me earlier?" He grinned. "Oh yeah, an 'old fossil.' But you are not alone. In fact, the vast majority of folks are just like you. Nobody wants to come to a class or listen to an old fossil. Why? It's not normal."

Jones held tightly to Baker's hand and inched his face a little closer. Talking softly but seriously, with an intensity that crackled in the air between them, Jones said, "If you ever listen to anything *anybody* tells you for the rest of your life, son, you'd better hear what I'm about to say . . .

"I am about to give you the fundamental anchor in a doctrine of extraordinary achievement that has seldom been revealed. For centuries this principle has been hidden. Yet it is hidden in plain sight. Deep within the truth of this law, power and worthlessness fight an unending battle for supremacy. The principle has great power because it is easily harnessed by anyone who chooses to do so. But the principle also bears the stain of worthlessness, for it is even more easily ignored. Will you harness the principle? Or will you ignore it? Listen carefully . . ."

Jones paused, took a deep breath, and began to speak the words that would one day change Baker's life and his legacy.

"If you are doing what everyone else is doing, you are doing something wrong. Why? Because most people are not obtaining results that are considered extraordinary.

"If your thinking is causing you to do what everyone else is doing, you are only contributing to the average. Even if you are contributing to the average at a high level, it is still . . . average.

"Do you want to be average? Do you want an average life span or an average lifestyle? Do you want an average marriage? Do you want to raise average children? Do you want an average spiritual life? Do you want average financial results? Do you want an average amount of influence for good in your community?

"No! Of course not! If you could wave a magic wand over your life, you'd create results in every part of your life that are wildly beyond the average. You would create results—you would create a life—that was extraordinary in every way.

"Therefore, in order to produce results that are wildly outside the average—to produce results that are extraordinary—you cannot afford to think like average people think. You cannot act like average people act. You cannot be what average people are . . . which is normal."

Jones's blue eyes gripped Baker for a few more seconds. He

wanted the words he had spoken to sink deeply into the younger man's heart and mind. The old man smiled finally and shook the hand he was already holding. Releasing, Jones cuffed Baker on the shoulder. "I will see you soon," he said. "Yes?"

"Yes," Baker replied.

With that, Jones turned to look around and get his bearings for the walk back to town. He waved and began to stride across the huge field, through wheat stalks reaching almost to his waist.

Baker watched him go for a moment, then turned away and began his own walk back to the truck. The farmer wasn't entirely sure what had just happened, but he felt different—better—than he had only thirty minutes ago. Baker wondered if he would really ever see the crazy old fellow again.

Reaching the truck, he opened the door before it occurred to him that he could have, and probably should have, offered Jones a ride back to Fairhope. It was not too late, Baker thought, but when he turned around and scanned the field in every direction, the old man was nowhere in sight.

The young farmer frowned. *Where could he have gone?*

Gradually a smile began to spread across Baker's face. Then he laughed out loud and climbed into the big F-150. He was still laughing as he turned the ignition; and when he shifted the truck into gear, Baker spoke out loud, "I don't know how you got out of the field that fast, old man. But however it happened . . . it sure wasn't normal."

Six

Kelli Porter held hands with Bart, her husband, as she looked across the bay from the passenger side of their white SUV. They were slowing momentarily, the VFW hall on their right, at the only caution light on Scenic Highway 98. "I'm thinking we'll be a bit early," Bart said. "That okay with you?"

"Fine with me," Kelli responded without turning her head. "How long will this last tonight?"

"I'm not really sure," Bart answered, accelerating the big vehicle to the south, away from town, along the charming two-lane highway.

Kelli's eyes remained focused on the broad expanse of water to their right and noted the position of the sun. It was 6:40 p.m., still a good forty-five minutes away, by her reckoning, from their local version of Canada's Northern Lights or Yellowstone's Old Faithful. It was a daily occurrence that transfixed locals and visitors alike. Sunset on Mobile Bay had become a signature event—a dazzling moment, when the huge, flaming ball of fire fell dramatically into the water.

"The kids are outside for sure now," Kelli murmured quietly.

Bart chuckled and squeezed his wife's hand. "We can turn around . . ."

"Nooo," she said, drawing out the word. Suddenly, she took a deep breath, exhaled just as quickly, and shifted a bit in the seat as if to reset her thoughts and focus. "I'm curious about this whole thing tonight. Even though it's going to kill me to be inside when the sun sets."

"We've lived here for fifteen years, Kelli. You haven't seen enough sunsets?"

They shot each other a quick grin as Bart slowed for another light. No words were necessary. Both knew the answer to that silly question.

For families like the Porters who live along the stretch of waterfront known as the Eastern Shore, sunset is a spectacle they rarely miss. People plan daily schedules around the time when they come out of their homes in the late afternoon to drive or bicycle or walk down to the bay. Folks greet each other like old friends (whether they recognize anyone or not) and enjoy the laughter of the children who play together in packs at the water's edge, soaking wet, splashing each other in their good clothes.

When the sun begins to approach the liquid horizon, a hush falls over the crowd. Waiting . . . waiting . . . all is silent until the very instant the object of the gathering dips its molten edge into the bay. When the sun touches the water, fifty or a hundred kids make a soft sizzling sound. *Ssss* . . . the sizzles dissolve into giggles, the giggles into laughter, and the laughter into a smattering of applause.

Kelli saw her future husband for the first time during their freshman year at Ohio State. He caught her eye in world history when the graduate assistant teaching the class mispronounced the phrase "for all intents and purposes." When the young professor said "for all intensive purposes," Bart shot a devilish grin across the aisle, and Kelli snickered out loud.

The uncontrolled laugh horrified Kelli but provided Bart the opening he had been seeking to approach the beautiful girl. Immediately after class, however, it had been Kelli who spoke first. She smiled and said, "*You* are bad."

Quick on his feet, Bart returned the smile and responded, "For all intensive purposes, that is probably very true."

By the end of the week, they were eating lunch together. At month's end they were dating. And by Christmas Bart knew they would be married one day. Kelli took a bit longer to convince, but when graduation rolled around several years later, the wedding date had been set.

The young couple relocated several times before finally settling, to the amazement of their friends, in what the rest of the country regarded as "the Deep South." Bart worked in an executive position as a financial analyst for a large insurance company in Nashville, Tennessee, while Kelli made use of her talent and skill as a freelance graphic artist.

On vacation after three years of marriage, they had driven down Interstate 65 all the way to Mobile, Alabama, and detoured through downtown Fairhope on their way to the beach. Enchanted by the variety of tiny shops and incredible restaurants scattered throughout the beautiful village, the couple never made it to the coast. And so it happened that during a few days of exploring, Bart and Kelli came to the conclusion that they wanted more than a visit. That very week they determined to move to Fairhope and, within six months, had actually done it.

Now a decade and a half later, Bart and Kelli were established residents. With three children under the age of twelve, Kelli had cut back considerably on her career in graphic design, but since most of the contacts, the correspondence, and even the actual work were done online, she still managed to create a significant addition to the family's income.

Bart simply changed locations and continued his work with the insurance company—the majority of what he did was online too. They were happy with each other, financially stable, and determined to be good parents. That particular desire to raise great kids was why, at that very moment, Bart and Kelli were walking across the parking lot toward the front entrance of the Grand Hotel.

"Tell me again who this guy is," Kelli said.

Bart took her hand and continued to walk. "Dear, I have told you everything I know. It was advertised at the bookstore. I heard, or I was told . . . well, they say he's an expert."

"On . . . ?" Kelli prompted.

"On? What do you mean, 'On?'" Bart asked, now a bit confused.

"On what? What is he an expert on? Whoever 'they' might be . . . *they* said he was an expert. So? An expert on what?"

"Well . . ." Bart was suddenly unsure. "Well, parenting, I guess."

"You guess?" Kelli's eyebrows lifted. She dropped Bart's hand and stopped walking. Facing him, she said, "You *guess* this man is an expert on parenting?"

"Kelli," Bart responded, exasperation seeping into his voice, "the guy is teaching a parenting class. So, yes, I *assume* he's an expert on parenting."

Kelli's first inclination was to grab the word "assume" and beat her husband over the head with it for dragging her to something he obviously knew nothing about. Instead, she nodded slowly and remained silent as they turned and entered the hotel. She was grateful to be married to a man so determined to be a great parent. This intense attention to anything regarding being a father, Kelli knew, was the result of Bart having grown up without one. His father had left the family, never to be seen again, six weeks before Bart was born.

The slow, quiet nod had the desired effect, Kelli noted to herself. Bart calmed quickly from what was about to become an argument. She had learned the slow-nod-with-silence method at a marriage class they had attended several years earlier. That class had been taught by a person, Kelli thought (but did not say aloud), who really had been an expert.

So who, she wondered as they walked toward the meeting room, *is this guy?*

Marriott's Grand Hotel was aptly named. The property's centuries-old oak trees and massive magnolias provide a backdrop for the exquisite, natural wood structure of the hotel. Fine dining, a fabulous spa, swimming pools, lakes, and a championship golf course are all part of why the Grand Hotel is a destination unto itself.

Less than five minutes down Scenic 98 from Fairhope, the Grand Hotel property is set on a prime piece of waterfront real estate known as Point Clear. Projecting westward into historic Mobile Bay, the point itself allows every guest an extraordinary and memorable view of stunning sunsets day after day, each more spectacular than the last.

Passing through the incredible hallways, the couple found the meeting location and walked in. Kelli strode purposefully to the only two chairs in the room. Attempting to ease the tension, she gestured dramatically and said to her husband, "Won't you join me? These are the last seats in the house, and we don't want to miss this. *They* say that the teacher is an expert." With that, Kelli sat down and patted the empty seat to her right.

Bart had no choice but to sit, and as he did, Kelli crossed her arms. "Okay, we're here," she said. "It's seven o'clock. What now?"

The "What Now" walked into the room seconds later. Jones was precisely on time, as he always was. Bart glanced to his left, and had he not been so bewildered himself, he might have laughed out loud at the horrified expression on Kelli's face.

Clearly, the old man was not what she had expected.

Seven

Jones was dressed as always, in jeans and a white T-shirt and wearing leather flip-flops. His snow-white hair was not messy, but neither was it brushed neatly. It was clean, however, and long enough to be finger combed easily from front to back and behind his ears on the sides.

"Good evening, Kelli. Hello, Bart." Jones welcomed the Porters by shaking their hands. Stepping back a few feet, he quickly sat down cross-legged on the floor in front of them and smiled. His blue eyes sparkled against the background of his dark skin and white hair as he announced, "My name is Jones. I am the teacher who has been chosen for this particular time in your lives."

Bart and Kelli had exchanged a look when Jones sat down on the floor. From the moment the old man entered the room, both were blindsided by the vast chasm that had instantly appeared between their expectations of a parenting class and whatever this reality was sitting in front of them. So taken aback were they in the moment that neither wondered until much later how the old man knew their names.

Jones placed his elbows on his knees and leaned forward. Still smiling, he said, "I trust that by the end of our time together, we will have uncovered treasure in forms and ways unimaginable to you right now."

Kelli reached for Bart's hand and took it without ever looking away from the old man.

"We have a few minutes before we begin the serious work," Jones said. "I'd love to hear just a bit about your family and your work. Do you mind? I know you have three children . . . what are their ages?"

"Pardon me," Bart said, "but how do you know anything about our children? Not to be rude . . ."

"Oh, I'm sorry," Jones said. "I didn't mean to make you uncomfortable. That is a beautiful charm bracelet, Kelli. Was it a gift?"

Kelli lifted her arm without thinking and stared briefly at the bracelet. The first thing that came to her mind was to tell the old man it was none of his business whether it was a gift or not. She wanted to ask what that had to do with anything and announce that she and her husband were leaving. Later she would wonder why she had not blurted out any of those things. There could have been any number of reasons, Kelli decided, but when the old man asked if the charm bracelet had been a gift, she answered, "Yes. It was a gift from Bart on our first anniversary."

"It's beautiful," Jones said. Looking to Bart, he appeared to change the subject. "Now then, you asked how I knew anything about your children . . . Things are easy enough to figure if a person gets in the habit of noticing."

They waited for him to continue, but Jones simply looked at them and remained quiet. Finally Bart asked, "And? What did you notice?"

The old man's smile broadened, and he said, "The charm bracelet. I noticed the charm bracelet. Lovely charms on it too. I'm sure there is an interesting story for each one. However, three of the charms, except for a slight shape variation and their color, are almost identical. They are baby shoes. *Three* baby shoes signifying your three children. By their shapes, color, and degree of wear, I believe your three children to be a boy and two girls. The boy is the oldest."

"Wow," Bart exclaimed, briefly staring openmouthed at the bracelet on his wife's wrist. "Okay. Well," he said as he gathered his wits. "I am a financial analyst. I work primarily with the insurance industry." Bart grinned and pretended to look at his hands and arms. "You might have already figured that out, though." They all laughed.

Kelli went on. "So, yes, we have three children. Art is twelve, and, yes, he's the oldest. Then the girls . . . Donna is ten. Our baby, Lucy, just turned five." Then she added, "Mr. Jones, you seem very familiar to me. Have we met?"

"First of all," the old man said, "call me Jones. Not Mr. Jones. Just Jones. And as for our having met . . . my guess would be that yes, at some point, surely we have run into each other." Without further explanation or even agreement from Kelli, Jones changed the subject again. "Our class is assembled," Jones stated as he slapped his palms crisply on his thighs. "It is eight minutes past seven o'clock—"

Bart looked at his watch and back at Jones, who continued to talk. He glanced at his wife and back at the old man before twisting in his chair. Bart looked directly behind himself, expecting to see a clock on the wall, but there wasn't one to be found.

After patiently enduring Bart's movement, Kelli placed her hand on his arm. She took this action while keeping her smile intact and her eyes on Jones—perfectly executing the sit-still maneuver that wives tend to use on their husbands and children.

Bart zoned back in as Jones said, "Sunset is at seven fifty-four this evening, but the sun will hit the water a bit earlier than that." To Kelli, he said, "I enjoy the sunsets too. Let's hold this evening's class outside." Kelli Porter was now as openmouthed as her husband had been the moment before.

As they stood, Jones moved toward the exit and added, "I say we convene on the end of the pier." The old man was already outside by the time the Porters reached the door. They shrugged at each other and hurried to follow.

Other than the old man, there was no one else around as Bart and Kelli made their way onto the wooden structure. Jones had stepped to the very end of the pier and, with his back to them, looked out across the bay, to the sun in the west, and spoke over his shoulder. "We won't stay long this evening. I suggest we use the sun's imminent farewell as a countdown of sorts."

He turned and faced the couple. There was a light wind that tugged at the old man's shirt and tousled his white hair. "There are now thirty-four minutes exactly," he said with an inkling of a smile, "before the bottom edge of our sun meets the horizon created by the water of this bay. Let us consider it a symbol of parental opportunity slipping through our fingers, never to be retrieved."

Motioning for Bart and Kelli to join him at the railing, Jones turned back around and was quiet again, this time for several minutes. The Porters waited uncomfortably. They felt it impolite at this point to say anything, but if they had talked to each other, one would have been sure to note that this was unlike any class—parenting or otherwise—either had ever experienced. "When one truly comprehends the fleeting nature of time," Jones finally said, "the urgency acknowledged often creates a greater degree of focus. We are thirty-one minutes from sundown."

The old man had leaned against the railing, his forearms flat against its top, and looked to his right. Kelli would remark later that it was as if he were gazing past the sun. "Twenty-eight minutes now," he said softly. "Watch it closely. The sun's movement is so much like the formative years of a child's life. Parents can become blind to the passage of time. We can also become blind to the truth of what's happening around us during that passage of time. We think we are paying attention, but the sun doesn't seem to move. So because nothing *seems* to be happening, we quickly become bored and look away. Only moments pass before we look back and realize that the sun—or our child—has moved significantly. Or is gone altogether.

"Twenty-seven minutes," Jones said and turned to look directly at Bart and Kelli. With his hands shoved comfortably into his pockets, he said, "It is my strong belief that far too many children have parents who try to do the best they can. Why are you here?"

Bart and Kelli exchanged an awkward glance. They didn't know where the old man was headed. *Why are you here? What kind of question is that?* they wondered, as subatomic particles of doubt began to sail unbidden from the couple who were beginning to wish they had not come.

"Bart? Kelli? You have three children," the old man began gently before tilting his head back and gazing at the sky as if he were trying to recall something just beyond his thoughts. "Art, who is twelve. Donna . . ." He smiled at Kelli. "You said Donna was ten . . ."

Kelli nodded a yes to Jones and took her husband's hand.

Jones, still smiling, finished with, ". . . and Lucy is five. Correct?"

Kelli and Bart nodded and leaned forward as if they were concentrating mightily. Bart took a deep breath, preparing to speak.

"Three quick questions," Jones said and held up three fingers, breaking in before Bart could begin whatever he was about to say. "This will only take a moment." Before either of the couple could reply, Jones put a single finger forward and asked, "As parents, do you believe that you are doing the very best you can and that you have endeavored to maintain that standard for more than twelve years now?"

The couple blinked, then looked at each other briefly before Kelli spoke. "Yes," she said, "I do. Obviously there is always room for improvement as parents. Um . . . I mean, as human beings we certainly want to improve . . . grow . . . that is, become better . . . or more effective . . ."

Kelli was searching, stumbling a bit, and she looked to her husband momentarily before hitting her stride. Her words poured out in a jumble but conveyed what she intended. "I do believe," she said, "that is, Bart and I believe together . . . I mean, with all the tools available to us as parents in the form of books and the most recent studies, that yes . . . yes, we are currently doing, and intend to continue doing, the very best we can." She lifted her chin, looked at Bart, who nodded, and focused again on Jones. "Yes," she stated once more. "We are."

"Good," Jones nodded agreeably. "I, too, believe that. I have all the confidence in the world that you are indeed doing the best you can."

He held up two fingers. "Second question. If society's best parents—the most loving, the most determined, the *most concerned* parents—are all raising their children by setting their sights on a target called 'doing the best we can,' is anyone aiming at the same thing?"

The strange question hung in the air for a minute as the couple—now not quite so certain—rolled it over in their heads. Bart and Kelli looked at each other searchingly for a moment before focusing again on the old man. "I don't know," Bart said at last.

"Care to hazard a guess?" They did not, so the old man continued with more of the question. "I believe most parents are not too different from you. I think most are probably doing the best they can. But what *is* that exactly? What guideline has society settled upon as the best method for bringing up kids? What do today's parents agree is the gold standard for raising children? Any clue?"

Bart looked as if he would have been happy to jump over the pier railing and swim for it. Kelli was lost as well. *What*, they wondered, *was wrong with doing the best you can? How could any parent do better than the best they could do?* As hard as they tried to fight it, the fingers of self-doubt were beginning to tap nervously in the minds of Kelli and Bart Porter.

What do today's parents agree is the gold standard for raising children? Unable to answer what seemed uncomfortably close to a personal challenge, the couple glanced at each other, keenly aware that they were the only attendees in a parenting class that had, so far, only managed to make them uncertain.

As they pondered the second question, Jones called out in a louder voice than he had been using, "Quit hiding over there!" The old man had an amused smirk on his face and was looking beyond the Porters. "If you intend to stay," he said, "the least you can do is come over here and help."

Bart and Kelli turned to see a man sitting in the pier's gazebo. As he rose to approach the small group, two things were obvious. First, by positioning himself below the gazebo railing and behind a large trash container, the man was clearly attempting to go unnoticed; and second, he was mortified to have been caught.

Seeing the embarrassment evident on the man's face, Jones cackled gleefully.

Eight

How had he seen me? I had walked out onto the pier when the old man and the couple had their backs turned. I was completely hidden behind the massive trash receptacle, and still, he had busted me.

Only a few days earlier I had been thrilled to see Jones in Fairhope. Since that unexpected meeting, I was very excited about the Thursday event and had planned my whole week around it. Anticipating the Grand Hotel's large ballroom would be packed with parents, I arrived early intending to get a good seat for the class. Unfortunately my cell phone rang as I pulled into the hotel parking lot.

The phone's screen read "Matt Baugher." It was my publisher. Just seeing his name there in my hand conjured up storm clouds of guilt that threatened to overwhelm me, but having not delivered my latest manuscript on time made it impossible to ignore his call. To some degree, I knew that my situation had also created professional problems for Matt. As the nonfiction publisher for one of the world's largest publishing companies, he had deadlines as well. So, as much as I wanted to find a hole to crawl into, as much as I wanted to run away, I answered the phone and talked with Matt for almost forty minutes.

When we finally said good-bye, I felt worse. For one thing, I knew that I was either very late for Jones's class or had missed it altogether, but the main reason for my mood was Matt. If he had yelled at me or threatened legal action, I could have taken it. But no, Matt was nice. He talked and laughed and assured me he was not worried in the slightest about my ability to deliver the best story we had ever done together. In other words, Matt was calm and cool. He was his usual upbeat, encouraging self, and though I don't think it was what he intended, I hung up the phone somehow feeling more pressure than ever.

I like Matt a lot and was horrified to be letting him down. Naturally, when I told him so, he said, "You're not letting me down," which I felt was more evidence that I was doing just that.

Then I couldn't find the parenting class. I checked every ballroom and was headed to the main lobby to ask for help when I glanced outside and saw Jones with only one couple. Disappointed that I had obviously missed everything, I headed for the pier. At least, I figured, I could still have a few minutes with Jones.

Arriving at the end of the wooden structure having not been seen, I heard a snippet of conversation that sounded serious and decided that I would not interrupt. I was sitting behind a large trash can half-trying to hear and half-trying not to hear when the old man called me out.

I stood, red-faced at having been discovered eavesdropping, but as I sheepishly approached the small group, Jones laughed, and somehow that made me feel better. He introduced me to the Porters, and after only a few minutes, my mood had changed entirely. Of course, Jones always made me feel better, but to some degree, my spirits were lifted because it was so interesting to watch someone else attempt to decode the old man.

It was immediately apparent that Bart and Kelli were mentally scrambling to figure out what they had gotten themselves into. From long experience, however, I knew something about Jones that, when I was in his presence, made me more patient with myself. It was something they were about to find out.

Through the years I had found that most conversations with Jones were a lot like gazing into those bizarre paintings in which one is supposed to be able to see the Statue of Liberty or an elephant or a face. At first, of course, one can't see anything at all. That result creates frustration leading to speculation about whether the entire exercise is a waste of time. Suddenly, however, all the clutter comes into dramatic focus, and one sees things clearly that were invisible only moments before.

The sun was behind the old man's left shoulder as he looked at me and winked. "Twenty-three minutes until sundown," he said. "I don't know if you were able to hear everything from behind the garbage can, but the question we are currently exploring is this: What do today's parents agree is the gold standard for raising children?"

Turning to Bart and Kelli, Jones nodded toward me and said, "He and his wife, Polly, have two boys. Who knows? Maybe he can help." Looking back to me, he grinned and added, "But help quickly, please. And let's sit down." With that, the old man stepped to the gazebo and grabbed a chair, moving it to face several others. "Come on," he said as he motioned for us to move faster. With a grin, Jones pointed to the sinking sun and added, "Twenty-two minutes."

Glancing at the Porters as we hurried over, I saw expressions of anxiety and confusion on their faces. Looking back to the old man, something bumped my memory, bringing to mind the many times I had watched Jones comport himself with total calm, perfectly happy as a deadline of one sort or another threatened ominously.

What was with the sunset countdown? I wondered as we arranged our chairs to face the old man. I understood the metaphor of the sun disappearing as it related to our children growing up and time running out on a parent's opportunity to affect their lives. I actually had been thinking about that a lot since Jones's observation about time in Fairhope several days earlier.

At this moment, however, Jones was after the answer to something else. He wanted to know what today's parents agree is the gold standard for raising children . . .

Jones's eyes twinkled when he realized that all three of us were staring at him. It was a look I had seen before. When I was a young man, that same expression had infuriated me. As my fear or anger or whatever escalated, he would match my desperation with his ability to become more composed, even tranquil. I remember wanting him to feel like me. I was upset. Why couldn't he be upset too? Then we could be upset together! *C'mon, Jones,* I would think, *be my friend!*

It took me years to understand that the old man was attempting to teach me something most people never learn: despite the ebb and flow of our feelings, we *can* control the way we act. "Patience, for instance," Jones once remarked, "is *not* a feeling. Patience is the description of a behavior. One can choose to act patiently even while the feeling of frustration tempts him to choose inappropriate behavior. It is impossible to feel frustrated and feel patient at the same time, but one can be inundated with feelings of frustration and still display patience. Patience is a discipline. It is an action. Patience is a chosen response."

I looked to the Porters, who didn't seem any closer to an answer than I was. Kelli sat to my right. She was the one in the middle, between her husband and me, directly facing Jones, whose back was to the bay. The sun, seeming larger by the minute as it moved ever closer to the horizon, was to his left.

Jones leaned back and crossed his arms behind his head. The old man's easy manner reminded me of every other time I had ever been around him. His temperament was absolutely imperturbable. While I was surprised at our collective inability to conjure up an answer to what, on the surface at least, seemed to be a fairly simple question, Jones displayed not an ounce of impatience or disappointment.

What do today's parents agree is the gold standard for raising children?

After allowing the growing sense of unease to drift through our tiny group, Jones lifted his hands in a helpless gesture of resignation. "Well," he began, "it's not a huge shock that an answer is not readily apparent. After all, even the most influential people rarely ponder the question we've raised. Unfortunately, when it *is* considered, our question is quickly dismissed by society as being unanswerable."

Jones shook his head and rearranged himself in the chair. Leaning forward, he said, "Knowing that the quality of our answers is always determined by the quality of our questions, think carefully about this particular one we have raised. What do today's parents agree is the gold standard for raising children?

"This is a good question." He paused. "Actually," the old man continued, "it's a *great* question. Yet any organization or expert who dares put forth any answer at all is rejected as presumptuous or ridiculed as intolerant. That answer—any answer—is labeled a matter of opinion, and as everyone knows, a matter of opinion can never be accepted as a standard for anything."

Jones took a deep breath and shrugged, exhaling in a sigh as he leaned back in his chair again. The old man looked away from us and toward the sun. In a softer, almost wistful voice, he said, "And so, very quietly, without anyone noticing, a tragedy is now in the process of playing out before our very eyes." Jones was quiet then, and I thought his expression odd, as if the tragedy he spoke of was personal somehow, as if it had hurt *him*.

Suddenly the old man was animated. He rose from the chair and passionately declared the conclusion to which he had come. "You see, my friends," he said, "by not addressing the issue of an *accepted* standard, today's parents have defaulted into an uncomfortable agreement with each other. They have agreed that there will *not* be a standard for raising our children.

"One set of parents teaches their daughter to say 'yes ma'am' and 'no sir.' Another couple contends *that* standard of behavior to be a matter of opinion.

"One parent demands her boys dress in trousers that are belted at the waist. Her boys must wear their ball caps with the bill pointed to the front, and those caps are to be removed, with no exceptions, when indoors. That parent's next-door neighbor, on the other hand, might have entirely different rules about what clothes her children are allowed to wear and how they are allowed to wear them. Meanwhile, society lives with increasingly discouraging results."

Kelli spoke. "So you are saying there are *no* standards?"

"Quite the contrary," Jones replied. "I am saying that there are *many* different standards. That is essentially why there is a vast array of parenting books published every year, each touting new methods or different ways to measure a child's success. There are scores of classes—most larger than this one—all being taught by a countless number of people who claim to be experts in the field of parenting."

"Jones?" a voice responded immediately. "Are *you* an expert in the field of parenting?"

The expression on Bart and Kelli's faces was one of mild shock and amusement. Evidently neither could believe Jones had been confronted in this manner. As for me, I *could* believe it. I was horrified, but I could believe it . . . because the words had come from my own mouth.

Yes, I was embarrassed. I was also familiar with the situation in which I had placed myself. Ever since the fifth grade I have been aware that my mouth occasionally leaps without warning from the resting position into unrestrained activity. More than once I have been as shocked as anyone else when fully formed sentences have vaulted from my throat toward a target well before any conscious thought was acknowledged in my mind.

Jones laughed at my outburst, and that alone was enough to make the Porters smile. "Am I an expert on parenting?" he repeated before answering. "No. No, I am not."

At that, the Porters stopped smiling. Kelli gave Bart a quick elbow, and that tickled Jones again, for he laughed even harder. "No, friends. Though I have 'parented' more than you could possibly imagine, I am here with you now, and perhaps a couple more evenings, to exercise for you my primary function."

"Which is?" Bart posed.

"You see, Bart . . . I work with people. I suppose you could say that people are a great passion of mine. But I have great interest in other things as well, and I can't help but notice the connections that exist. For instance, try this. In a way people are like trees."

When all three of us furrowed our brows at the same time, Jones laughed. "Yep," he continued, "folks are a lot like trees. You can know them by their fruit. You see, everyone produces one kind or another. In an orchard a quick examination of a piece of fruit can reveal a lot about the health of the tree. Without looking at the limbs, measuring the base, or inspecting the leaves, a single apple or pear can often tell you exactly what you need to know."

After a pause the old man sat back down and crossed his arms comfortably. "Here's an example . . . The Meyer lemon is a hybrid," he said, "and should ripen in this area around the middle of November. If one happens upon a mature tree during that time, even having never seen it before, one can easily discern how the tree has been 'raised.' Kelli? You look like a citrus person. Isn't that correct?"

"Well . . . yes," Kelli replied hesitantly. It was not because she disagreed but because she did know something about citrus and couldn't figure out exactly what made her "look like a citrus person." She glanced at me as if I could explain Jones, but I was useless, having given up on that possibility several decades earlier.

Still without a clue as to where this line of questioning might be taking them, Kelli gamely plowed ahead. "We have a couple of orange trees, along with a Satsuma and three Meyer lemon trees in our yard. One of them is huge and was there when we moved in. It was obviously never cared for. It took me several years to get it blooming and bearing fruit. It'll never be right, though."

Jones tilted his head knowingly but asked the question anyway. "Why do you say it will never be right, Kelli?"

As she answered, Bart and I eased back in our chairs. Kelli said, "The big tree won't ever be what it could have been because the previous owners of the house never took care of it. The tree just grew kind of . . . well, uncontrolled for years before I ever had a chance with it. It's fine now. Or okay, I guess. But that tree is huge and doesn't produce nearly the fruit of my other two trees, and they are barely more than five years old."

"And they're the same kind of tree?" I asked. "Hybrid Meyer lemons? We have citrus trees in our yard and have several of those too."

Kelli nodded. "Yes, same kind of tree. The two Meyer lemons that are doing so well were just small, staked plants when I bought them from Home Depot five years ago. Only cost me fifteen dollars apiece, but last year, we got more than a hundred lemons from each tree."

I was impressed and told her so, but Jones, always delving deeper, had another question. "Kelli," he said, "why did the young trees turn out so well? How did you know what to do?"

Kelli was excited and a bit proud that she had been the first to understand the point of the old man's story. She had also figured out how it linked to what they had already discussed. Slowly, as if revealing the location of a treasure, she said, "I knew what to do with the trees . . . because . . . I followed the directions! I never thought about it this way, but when I took my tiny lemon trees home from the store, I carried with me a sheet of paper that Home Depot had provided. Printed on that single page were *specific* directions. They are the same directions everybody gets when they buy a Meyer lemon tree at Home Depot. They are the same . . . because they work. And they work every time. The directions basically say that if you do this, you will get that. Why? How do they know for sure? Well, I'm guessing it is because all the Meyer lemon experts in the world have spent years and years sharing information and figuring out the very best way to grow Meyer lemon trees . . ."

Kelli stopped speaking and with a huge grin added the final piece of the puzzle. It was the whole point of Jones's diversion into trees, then lemon trees specifically, in the first place. She had understood it and now wanted to make sure that Bart and I were on board as well. "Based upon years of great results, citrus growers have now *agreed upon a single standard*. That one standard, having been in place and adhered to now for many years, is responsible for generations of incredibly productive trees."

Growing serious, Kelli narrowed her eyes in thought. Pointing her finger approvingly at Jones, she said, "This man is telling us that at least one reason our society does not consistently produce awesome results in the lives of its children is because we have not agreed upon a standard by which they will be raised."

Satisfied, Kelli dipped her head once at us and sat back in her chair to face Jones. "Very nice," Jones nodded with approval. "Very nice." Then, with a new intensity, he said, "Now . . . I want you to think carefully here . . . At the very beginning of the initial quest for a standard on raising Meyer lemon trees, what was the first decision that had to be agreed upon?"

Concentrating, Bart quickly threw out an answer. "Somebody had to say what they were after."

"Go on," Jones urged.

"I'd suppose the first thing someone had to do was to agree on the lemons . . . the actual fruit. Did they want big lemons or little ones? Did they want their trees to produce bitter lemons, like those already sold at supermarkets? Obviously that answer was no because if you eat a Meyer lemon, there's no bitterness in the flavor. Instead, there is a recognizable hint of sweetness. Meyers aren't horribly sour like most lemons. So, from the beginning, someone had to state for the record—and convince others to agree upon—the particular result they wanted to achieve.

"And so it follows," Bart said with a new respect for the old man in front of him, "that when we set out to accomplish something without a specific, agreed-upon result, that lack of a common target yields results that are unpredictable at best."

"That is correct," Jones said. "By the way, there are eleven minutes now until the sun touches the water. We have just enough time to answer the third question.

"What results do you want with your children? Ten years from now . . . or seven years or fifteen years . . . when your children become adults . . . when at last you inspect the fruit of the tree you have pruned and fertilized and watered for years . . . what fruit do you want to see?"

"Can we make a list?" Kelli asked and, not waiting for a reply, answered herself. "Yes, you can make a list." Digging a pen and small pad from her purse, she said, "I am putting down a great education as number one."

"Consider that answer carefully before you write anything in ink," Jones cautioned, and Kelli looked up with a frown.

"As important as a great education may be," Jones explained, "that is not an end result. We all know highly educated people who are deep in debt or even unemployed. So while an education might *lead* to a result for your child, it is not *the* result itself. I urge you to list the actual results you want for your child."

"Physically? Mentally?" Bart probed. "Emotionally?"

"Yes," Jones replied. "What results in every one of those areas do you desire for your children when they leave the nest?"

"To have a job," Bart offered.

"To be able to get a job if they want one," Kelli said, amending the definition somewhat. "And I say 'if they want one' because Art is twelve and already talking about owning a business."

"He'll need common sense. Wisdom. And he'll have to be confident," I said. "Put that down."

"Confident, yes," Kelli clarified, "but not arrogant."

"That's true," I agreed. "Add humble."

In no time at all we had added financially astute, good manners, and quite a few others. We grew increasingly excited as we reexamined and prioritized our results and began to understand that we were producing an excellent diagram of the adults we desired our children to become.

Our ideas were just beginning to slow when Jones announced, "I will be at this very place one week from this evening. Again, we will start at seven o'clock. We will discuss how to choose and implement the specific processes that will produce the results we've listed this evening. Any questions?" There were none, so he said, "We have ninety seconds until the sun meets the water." He stood, gestured to the west, and said, "Let's enjoy this."

Jones moved toward the pier's wooden railing but stopped several feet short of it, standing instead in the middle of the structure with his hands on his hips, looking out across the bay. We joined him but moved all the way to the railing, dazzled as always by the incredible sunset happening before our very eyes.

I knew the tradition, of course, but was delighted to hear my new friends do the sizzle sound as the sun "touched" the bay. I laughed and sizzled, too, caught up in the moment and happy to be there.

When the sun disappeared, I shook hands with Bart and told Kelli that my wife, Polly, would be with me next week. When I asked which room the class was held in, they gave me a funny look and explained that the addition of my wife the following week would increase our enrollment by 25 percent.

I must confess that I was having a hard time fully grasping the concept of a "class" with only four people in it. Nonetheless, I said my good-byes and almost laughed out loud as the Porters turned to go. Realizing Jones was no longer there and unavailable to thank for what had turned out to be an interesting evening, Bart and Kelli were surprised by his disappearance. Me? I had expected as much and had noticed the old man was gone the instant we turned around.

I stayed at the pier's end, with my back and elbows resting on the railing, as they walked to the gazebo, stopping there to collect Kelli's purse. Polly and the boys were out of town; therefore, I was in no hurry to get home and thought I would stay awhile to see if any speckled trout showed up after dark. Most docks and piers on the bay had floodlights aimed at the water from mounts under the structure. Many nights the anglers who fish the lights see the trout and redfish long before they ever catch one.

As I watched, it became apparent that something had captured the Porters' attention, for they had stopped in the gazebo.

From my vantage point it seemed as if the couple was staring at the chairs. They stood motionless for a long moment before stepping close enough for Bart to reach out his hand, extend his forefinger, and touch the seat of the chair.

Actually, he had touched something *on* the chair, a fact that became clear as first Bart, then Kelli reached out, each delicately picking up a tiny item from the seats they had occupied a short time earlier. Both used a thumb and forefinger to hold an object up into the light for examination. Whatever they had, I thought, was too small for me to identify from the railing.

I didn't walk over but continued to watch carefully. I could see that neither of them knew what to make of this tiny object. Bart looked around to find me and held something up in his hand. With a big grin, he spoke loudly, saying, "It's a lemon seed!" and shrugged. Pointing to Kelli, he added, "She has one too." Kelli held it up for me to see, and Bart added, "Now that I think about it, I will bet you every dollar you have in your pocket right now that it is a *Meyer* lemon seed."

We were still the only folks on the pier. Bart took a few steps toward me and said, "I've got to say . . . this Jones guy is very different. I like him. I like him a lot. But he is very . . . ah . . . different."

You don't know the half of it, I thought. Aloud, I said, "Yes, he is," and laughed lightly.

I stayed by the rail while the couple gathered their things and, after promising to see me the following week, waved good-bye. Before getting too far down the walkway, Kelli turned around and addressed me in a loud voice. "Hey . . . you have one too. A lemon seed, I mean. It's on your chair, so get it before you leave, okay?" I said that I would and waved my thanks.

When at last I was alone, I stared out at the bay and barely saw the swirls of darkening color in the sky. Feeling the goose bumps rise on my neck and arms, I wondered, *What now? Where is all this headed?* I said a quick prayer and turned. The pier was deserted, darkness encroaching across the salty water. I looked up. Only the glow of a sodium-vapor bulb cut through a night made thicker by the mist and humid air. It all seemed too familiar, of course.

At my chair I stopped to pick up what had been placed in the middle of the seat. Cupping the object in my palm, I studied it carefully and thought about how much I valued this one tiny seed simply because Jones had left it for me. It seemed an amazing representation of the first seeds the old man had planted in my life so many years ago.

I smiled to myself, eased it into my pocket, and walked into the night.

Nine

A principled process—one that produces as it is intended every single time—can be created only when the final result desired is clearly defined."

"So a person should always focus on the result?" the young woman asked.

"No," Jones replied. "Not at all. I am saying only that the end result must be determined before an effective process can be put in place to achieve that result. However, once that process is in place, one has only to adhere to the process—those daily steps—that lead inevitably to the final result."

Christy Haynes was naturally talkative, and the old man she had run into was not short of anything to say either. In her early thirties, she was the young wife of a minister and the mother of three children. Having arrived early for what she had determined was a networking opportunity, Christy walked the grounds of the Grand Hotel and met an old man with a charming personality. He had called her by name, which was not really surprising. After all, she worked as a photographer and often accompanied

Brady, her husband, on church youth trips. A lot of folks knew Christy, and every one of them loved her greatly.

She was tall and thin with long, dark hair. She was beautiful, but Christy's bubbly personality was the first thing anyone noticed. As a photographer who never posed anyone, her ability to connect immediately with the people she photographed created a relaxed, joyful atmosphere that was always visible in the final product. It was her talent, however, that made Christy's clients gasp when they saw themselves in her photos.

Christy had a gift with natural light. She not only didn't pose her clients but also never used extra lighting or flash equipment either. Whatever it was that Christy was able to see wasn't visible to anyone else . . . but the camera caught it. Her photographs were proof of some sixth sense that never seemed to fail.

Christy enjoyed her work but knew she needed better equipment to produce the magic she really saw. One reason she wanted to produce the very best was her love for people. Because she loved people and saw her work as a way to encourage others, Christy wanted her clients to see themselves the way she did. Consistently her subjects would gaze at a photograph knowing they had never looked better in their lives.

Though her talent was huge, Christy's business was not. As the wife of a minister, she was used to starting over in new towns. As the mother of three children, she was often involved in more than the ordinary person could handle, but Christy was not ordinary, and she was determined to wring every last drop out of life. If that meant helping Brady with the youth group, photographing clients while the kids were in school, and being transportation for art and soccer, all the while searching for new business, so be it. She was happy, and her family was happy too. The only real challenge they faced was financial. Money, as was the case with many young families, was tight. Money, for a minister's family, was tighter than for most.

Christy was constantly on the lookout for luncheons or classes or gatherings of one kind or another. Those events were great for meeting potential clients, and, in fact, it had been a client who had mentioned the class for which she was waiting. That client was Kelli Porter.

Kelli had been in awe of the portraits Christy had produced of her children, and because (for the first time in their lives) the kids had enjoyed the session, she determined to keep up with this particular photographer. Kelli had already recommended her to several friends, and when she called Christy to tell her, Kelli also mentioned the class she and Bart were attending.

When Christy had asked about the class and its teacher, Kelli had been unsure how to answer. She mentioned parenting and life skills and something about a plan for "when our kids are grown." Kelli also mentioned that the teacher was an expert, but she had to get off the phone before Christy could find out more.

In reality, it hadn't really mattered to Christy what the class was about or who taught it. She was chiefly interested in the access she would have to all the people in the class. There would probably be several hundred there, she knew. After all, the class was being held at the Grand Hotel.

When Christy asked the old man if he was a guest at the hotel, she was somewhat surprised to hear that he was the expert who taught the class she had come to attend. He certainly didn't seem like a typical teacher to Christy. The old man told her that everyone would gather at seven on the end of the pier. At least that made sense. *What a great location*, Christy thought, *for a time to get to know a few others in the class before it began.*

"I'm a little different in my approach to life," she had said to the old man as an answer to one of the several questions he had asked. It was true. Christy had grown up in an environment where everyone was expected to be and act and think the same. She wasn't a contrarian, but friends and family had always described her with an old cliché. "Christy," they would say, "marches to the beat of her own drum," and that is precisely why she was excited when the old man told her that "being a bit different" was a requirement in order to accelerate personal and professional growth.

When asked to explain, Jones said simply, "Everybody wants to make a difference, but nobody wants to be different. And you simply cannot have one without the other."

Christy laughed out loud.

When the old man had revealed himself as the teacher of the class, Christy asked about the subject matter. "What would you like to learn?" the old man responded.

"Oh, my!" Christy said and threw her arms in the air. "There's so much I want to learn. We don't have much money, but we have three great kids. I want to be a better mom, a better person, better wife, photographer, businessperson . . ." She paused and said, "I can list everything if you want."

Jones chuckled and told her about the importance of process, principles, and results. They discussed how each had its place and why each was necessary. Before pointing her to the pier and assuring her that he would be along in a bit, the old man said, "You are one of a kind, and that is a very good thing. You should remember that and act like you know it. Operate at the very edge of becoming every part of everything you are supposed to be."

At my wife's insistence we arrived early for the second parenting class. Polly and I ate dinner in the Saltwater Grill and kept an eye out for Jones. After our meal we had thirty minutes to kill before the class was scheduled to begin. Remembering that we would again convene on the pier, I suggested a quick stroll around the Grand Hotel property that would meander in that general direction. We crossed by the charming lake with its fountains and waterfalls and soon passed one of the conspicuous No Fishing signs. The sign caused us to laugh as we thought about our boys who, during every visit to the hotel, would threaten to sneak out at night and "catch those monsters" they could plainly see from the bank. I did my Austin/Adam impression for Polly. *Please, Mama. Nobody will know. Please. Only once, okay? Okay? Did you see the fish? Mama, please. Please . . .*

"I'm still looking for Jones to maybe arrive early," Polly said as we walked away from the pond. She reached over to take my hand and squeezed it. "You know?" she added and wiggled her eyebrows at me when I looked to see if she was serious. She was.

Dramatically rolling my eyes in response, I stopped and declared, "Dear. In all the years I have known this man, yes, I have seen him show up unexpectedly many times. However . . . and this is a big, five-hundred-pound 'however'—listen to me now—every *single* occasion upon which he has ever stated a time to meet or to arrive or whatever . . . Jones did not vary fifteen seconds from the exact time he set. I'm telling you, dear, the man's gonna walk onto the pier at seven o'clock and not a minute earlier or later."

I knew she would not be able to help herself. She could not. "But if it were somehow *possible*—"

"Walk," I interrupted. "Dear. Please. Please. Just walk."

Polly gritted her teeth and theatrically squeezed my hand with both of hers, hard, as if she were so aggravated she might just pinch my hand in two. We both laughed, and I asked, "Are you through?"

"Yes," she said sweetly and patted my hand before giving it back to me.

"Okay," I said, now taking her hand in mine. "Walk." We eased through the trees by the Spa Building, heading for the brick pathway that would take us along the water and around the point to the pier.

As we matched steps, Polly said, "On."

I glanced at her. "What?"

"On," she said again.

"On what?"

"You said 'walk.' I said, 'on.'"

"Oh," I responded with a nod. "I got you."

"Isn't that what you told me Jones would say?"

"Yep." I smiled. "I haven't thought about that in a while. I mean, I have the principle tucked firmly into my everyday life, but the way he would say it . . ." I chuckled at the memory.

"Tell me," Polly demanded. "While we're walking. Can you?"

"Well . . ." I thought for a minute.

When I had first met the old man years before, one of his most consistent lessons was what, to me, outwardly appeared to be an incredibly ordinary message: *walk on*. He'd say, "Son, the biggest part of wherever you end up in life is gonna be determined by the choices you make when things get tough. And trust me," he'd say, cocking his head and peering through his bushy, white eyebrows, "when everybody's crying and saying, 'What do we do now?' you'll be halfway home just by answering the question correctly. The answer, son, is 'walk on.'"

That simple thought, that direction about what to do even when things are falling apart, eventually became the crucial Seventh Decision in my first novel, *The Traveler's Gift*. "Walk on!" Or as the Seventh Decision states: "I Will Persist Without Exception!"

Back then—now, too, as far as I know—Jones actually did walk everywhere he went. Therefore, sensing that I was receiving life-altering information, I joined the old man whenever I could. As I trotted beside him on the beach or on a road, he would often make me laugh by saying those two words over and over again, matching his voice to the beat of his steps. Walk. On. Walk. On. Walk on, brother. Walk on, sister. Walk. On. Walk. On.

Polly glanced at her watch. "Still ten minutes away . . ."

For lack of anywhere else to go right then, we stayed in the same spot. Keeping our eyes on the time and the pier, I pointed out our classmates, the Porters, when they arrived and told her what little I knew about them. Bart and Kelli were the only ones on the wooden structure at the time, and we were in a beautiful location between two oaks. I was in no hurry to join them and was in fact intending to "pull a Jones" myself and walk onto the pier at seven o'clock on the dot.

Polly looked away from the pier and to the west, toward the water's edge past the marina. Shielding her eyes from the sun, she said, "Wouldn't you give anything to see a jubilee?"

"Yes," I said, now shading my eyes and looking in the same direction. "Well, almost anything. I've heard about them all my life. And remember? A long time ago I talked to that guy who found one and was right in the middle of it for over an hour? What made you think of a jubilee?"

Polly turned away from the sun and shrugged. "I don't know. I think about jubilees every time we come over here, don't you?"

Nodding slowly, I considered the question and agreed. "You know, it never really occurred to me that I did, but now that you mention it, I guess I do. Yeah," I said, nodding again. "I do. I give at least a passing thought to the possibility of a jubilee every time I'm on the Eastern Shore."

Polly and I aren't the only ones who think about it. In the

Baldwin County area of Alabama, one needs only to toss the topic of a jubilee into any conversation in order to spend the next several hours listening to stories about the phenomenon. A typical jubilee—there might be two, sometimes three, occurrences per year—will deliver flounder, shrimp, and crab by the tons to some random segment of a small but precise piece of coastline on the Eastern Shore. The entire expanse in which every one of these events have occurred for hundreds of years is bounded by Point Clear at the southern edge and just above Daphne to the north. Totaling a mere fifteen miles, it is the only place in the world where this happens regularly. A jubilee materializes unannounced, usually between 3:00 and 5:00 a.m., and without warning of any kind.

After centuries of these annual events, jubilees are now known to be a result of salinity stratification—a layering effect of the heavier, saltier water from the Gulf of Mexico to the south overlain by the lighter, fresh water swept into the bay by rivers from the north. This causes an upwelling of oxygen-poor water that pushes crustaceans and bottom fish to the shore by the tens of thousands.

The sea creatures are seemingly stunned and unable to swim. They lie quietly in the shallowest of water surrounded by vast numbers of their own kind until, at last, the tide shifts, and the jubilee is over. At that time they "wake up," no worse for the experience, and swim back into deep water. But there is a window—maybe an hour or ninety minutes—when all the shrimp, crab, and flounder that can be hauled away are easily gathered by anyone lucky enough to be there at that perfect point in time.

Luck. It does seem to be the only common denominator between those relatively few people who have been fortunate enough to witness what is surely one of nature's most puzzling and utterly obscure spectacles. Consider the odd fact that in the entire world, there is no other natural display that can be compared to this bizarre, recurring, but irregular event.

While today we exist in an era when nothing seems inconceivable, when every material experience appears to be obtainable, even now, no one can reserve the opportunity to see a jubilee. There is no ticket one can buy, no favor that can gain admission. Neither wealth nor fame, scientific research nor mathematical equation, physical sacrifice nor the intervention of federal government can produce a single shred of hope that one might be able to schedule the date or hour and plan to attend an upcoming jubilee, for they have proven impossible to predict and always take place in the dead of night.

Tales and records of jubilees have been passed along for generations as a colorful part of the Eastern Shore's history that predates the region's European settlement. First identified and mapped by Spanish explorers, this natural harbor, known for its unusual bounty, was originally called Bahia del Espiritu Santo— the Bay of the Holy Spirit. It is still an apt name for a body of water that regularly produces miracles.

We were standing at the base of one of the oaks, facing the water and the pier, far enough away not to have been noticed by Bart or Kelli, when I felt a hand on my shoulder. Surprised, I turned to find Jones practically in between us. His other hand was on the shoulder of my wife. "Hello, you two," he said. "Polly, it's so good to see you."

We hugged him and expressed our appreciation for his time and for the opportunity to experience the parenting class.

"It's different, isn't it? The class?" Jones asked. At least I supposed he was asking. I figured he surely had to know that, yes, anything in which he was involved was, by definition, different.

"I know I'm a little early," Jones said, "but I thought we would talk for a few moments before we join the others." When he mentioned the others, Jones had stepped forward and looked out at the end of the pier. Polly used that precise instant to duck behind the old man and stick out her tongue at me. Being the adult in the situation, however, I kept quiet and did not say anything in front of Jones about her conduct.

I stood by as Jones asked Polly about the boys, about the house, local news, and friends in Orange Beach. Watching my wife, who smiled a bit too delightfully at me several times while they talked, one would have thought that Jones's premature arrival allowed hours and hours of extra conversation. But no, they talked for about five minutes, and very soon I noted out loud for their benefit that it was time to head to the pier.

Jones offered Polly his arm, she took it, and I followed along behind as they walked toward the water. "I hope you enjoy this tonight," I heard him say.

"I'm sure I will," Polly answered before glancing mischievously at me and adding a question for the old man. "Jones, along with the parenting material, might you include some instruction for husbands?"

"Yes," Jones said as he stepped onto the pier. "It will be difficult to do, but I promise to make the attempt." Stopping, he leaned toward her and spoke softly but so that I could hear as well. "Maybe I shouldn't promise, though. We only have an hour, and as you know, husbands can be a dim lot." Jones looked at me and smiled.

Then he laughed loudly and turned, striding purposefully toward the end of the pier, leaving me to make that long walk with my beautiful and overly amused wife.

Ten

Jones was already greeting Bart and Kelli by the time Polly and I made it to the end of the pier. At a glance I saw that five chairs had been arranged in a semicircle. I assumed one was for Jones, but as I was introducing Polly to the Porters, a young woman arrived and was greeted enthusiastically by the old man.

"Christy!" Kelli exclaimed and hurried over to give the newcomer a hug. Within seconds Kelli was back with her friend. Introductions were made, and when the ladies began talking, Bart and I drifted out of the group at the same time and moved to the rail together.

"Polly seems great," Bart said without looking my way. "She's very nice." He was closely watching the three women.

"Thanks," I answered. "So is Kelli." My eyes never left the same scene.

"Thank you," Bart said. "Kelli is awesome." He paused. We watched. They talked. "I'm sure Polly is awesome," Bart said.

"Yes," I answered as if on remote control, "she certainly is."

After another moment of silence between us, Bart asked, "How do they do that?"

"I don't know," I replied, "but wouldn't you like to be able to do it?"

"Mm-hm," Bart responded as he nodded. "I would be president of the United States with that talent. Or at least the richest man in Texas."

"You guys moving to Texas?" I asked.

"Only if I can figure out how women do that," he said, still watching intently. "Then I could probably buy Texas."

"Congratulations, then," I said, chuckling. "Fairhope is a charming place, and you've cemented yourself as a lifetime resident."

Husbands around the world rarely talk openly about a conclusion to which most of them have come. It is simply that men—especially married men—are in awe of a woman's ability to size up a person in seconds. Incredibly, females of our species are able to decide instantly and accurately whether or not the person they have just met is worthy of more than a handshake.

Most men quietly believe that complicated trials would be over in minutes if the legal system would simply ban men from jury duty. With women in charge, men assert, court dockets around the world could be cleared in a matter of days. If twelve ladies were positioned in the jury box, the bailiff could trot out the accused for a few handshakes, a bit of small talk, and not five minutes would pass before the women would know with certainty whether to free the unjustly accused or send that dirtbag to jail. Either way, justice would be swift and true.

Men envy the gift of discernment their wives possess, but they are often confused by their conclusions. For the uninitiated (a new husband), the presentation of a conclusion by his wife can be maddening.

"What did you think?" the man might ask after having introduced his wife that evening to their new investment counselor. "Chuck's a great guy, isn't he?"

"No," the woman replies. "He is *not* a great guy, and there is no way in the world you are letting him anywhere near our money."

The husband, having known Chuck for weeks or months, is flabbergasted and moves immediately into what most men consider a logical line of questions. "Why do you say Chuck is not a great guy? You only drank coffee with the man. You've known him for all of ten minutes. How could you possibly know anything about him? Specifically, what is it that you don't like about Chuck?"

"I don't know," she says, adding only, "but I am absolutely sure about this." The conversation is always over at this point, occasionally because the man has run away screaming, in search of the nearest cliff from which he can jump.

Deep within us, however, no matter how much men protest, we are truly in awe. A quick glance at my wife during the hand-shaking part of the introduction and I knew that Polly liked Christy and Kelli instantly. Especially Christy.

We took our seats with Christy in the middle chair. Polly was to her right and Kelli to her left. Bart and I sat on each end of the tiny row beside our respective wives. While Jones was arranging himself cross-legged on the pier deck, Bart caught my attention. With a quizzical expression on his face, he patted his chair and held up five fingers. I nodded, seeing he had now noticed what I had spotted earlier. There were five people attending class that evening and exactly five chairs set *in advance*, one for each.

"Ladies," Jones said to Polly and Christy, "I believe a brief introduction is in order. Please, would you do us the honor?"

The two looked at each other and laughed. "Well, I'm Christy Haynes," she said. "I'll go first. I live in Orange Beach. My husband is a minister. I am a photographer, and we have two boys and a little girl."

I looked more closely at this new arrival from our home-town. Following my wife's lead, I liked her immediately. She appeared to be of Italian descent (or Greek, maybe?) and owned a mischievous smile that matched her personality. That bright disposition, I suspected, went a long way with her family . . . and everyone else with whom she came in contact.

My wife said, "I'm Polly Andrews"—she half-turned to Christy—"and we live in Orange Beach too." Again speaking to the group, she grinned, patted me on the leg, and said, "I am his keeper." That made everyone laugh, and Polly finished with comments about the ages of our two boys.

Jones smiled and slapped his hands. Rubbing them together briskly, he began. "Christy, Polly . . . as you know, this is our second meeting. Last week we decided that in order for all of us to agree upon a consistent way of parenting—a standard—we must first identify and then agree upon the ultimate results we wish to see in our children when they become adults.

"For instance, if you, Christy, desire financial independence for your children, but Kelli cares only that they know how to exist by panhandling for food, the operating procedure for each parent to achieve that result would be different. In other words, there would be no standard. Christy and Kelli would then exist, as most of today's society does, as two parents who had agreed to disagree.

"Without specific results as a target—results that are agreed upon in advance—most parents simply yield to 'doing the best we can,' which is not a standard. That lack of a specific objective yields less than satisfactory results. Do you understand?"

Christy, Polly, and the rest of us indicated that yes, we understood. "Good. Kelli, do you have the list we made last week?" She held it up, prompting Jones to ask, "Will you read it for us, please?"

Kelli called out the list slowly as we all scribbled down our own copies. There were twenty results on that list. The week before, Kelli, Bart, and I had agreed upon each of them.

They were:

1. To be divinely guided
2. To possess great wisdom, understanding, and common sense
3. To have a grateful spirit
4. To have a joyful spirit
5. To be financially astute
6. To be responsible
7. To be a person of good morals
8. To be loyal
9. To have a great and abiding faith
10. To have good manners
11. To be humble
12. To be hardworking
13. To be confident
14. To be honest
15. To be healthy and physically fit
16. To have great friends
17. To have a respect for authority
18. To have a servant's heart
19. To be a creative thinker
20. To accept the role of a leader, effectively demonstrating and guiding others to the results listed above

Jones waited for us to finish writing and said, "Any questions? Before we move forward, examine them closely. Remember, if one intends to create an agreed-upon standard by which children should be raised, the end result you are after must be thoroughly explored. Only the end result you desire will reveal what must be done in the present—a standard operating procedure—in order to reach that specific result in the future."

The old man waited as we examined the list. After a time he instructed us to look at number seven, which we did. There were no comments at all, prompting Jones to remark, "'To be a person of good morals' is a bit ambiguous, don't you think? I believe we need to be more specific. There are results you can place on this list that will cover 'morals' more efficiently than the actual word. In addition, they encompass much firmer ground than mere 'good morals' could ever hope to accomplish as a target."

Jones was patient, but when he saw that our tiny group was not closing in on the answer, he gave it to us. "Why don't we try *integrity* and *character*?" he asked. "And list them separately."

Looking up from his notes, Bart asked, "Separately? Aren't integrity and character virtually the same things?"

"What do you think?" Jones asked us. "Integrity and character? Are they really different words for the same thing?"

After a bit of hesitation, looking to each other for support, we agreed. Were integrity and character the same? Yes, they were. Practically identical. I had already begun to erase *integrity* from my list when Jones said, "No. Neither is the same. Both words have entirely different meanings. In order for you to adequately instill integrity and character, it would behoove each of you to know exactly what that difference is."

I was used to this kind of thing with Jones. I had seen him excavate hearts and minds that few had ever been able to reach. The old man could dig deep, rooting out the garbage of misconceptions or flat-out bad thinking . . . and do it faster than most folks recognized it being done.

That's what he did. Every day and all the time. I remember once when a lady asked Jones what kind of work he did, he told her he was an Inclinational Archaeologist. When she asked what that was, he said he specialized in "the excavation of thoughts by which living subjects were inclined to do great things." She had no clue what he meant, of course, but I did. Jones's conversations were designed to reveal a pattern of decisions that eventually unearthed one's very thinking.

Polly looked at me for reassurance. *All good?* she wanted to know. I gave her a little smile and nod. As I looked at the faces of the others, I could see that they were concentrating intently. Bart had his arms crossed, but not in a closed-off way. His expression was one of interest and expectation, as if he was enjoying a mystery on television.

"Integrity. To have integrity," Jones began, "is to be trustworthy and reliable, capable of performing the task for which it was created. A bank can have integrity. A bridge or a fire escape can have integrity. A person can have integrity too. That person is trustworthy, reliable, and capable of performing the tasks for which he was created. He is *capable* of performing those tasks.

"Morality is different. Morality can be exhibited by a person who is not doing what is wrong." Jones paused to be sure we were following closely. "A moral person does not lie or steal. But a person can be moral by doing nothing. One can stay in bed all day and remain moral.

"Now," Jones said, scooting closer to us, "while morality is not doing what is wrong, character is actively doing what is right. For instance, a person who sees a wrong being done but does not participate in that activity is still a moral person. He did nothing wrong. But to speak up, rather than turn away from an injustice, requires character. Therefore, without the spine to do what is right, it is possible to be a moral person with weak character.

"This, of course, leads us to the logical conclusion that a person without morals cannot be a person of character. Why? For the simple reason that it is impossible to do what is right while doing what is wrong. Therefore, it stands that a person who cheats at golf or on a spouse, a person who misleads or steals, is not and cannot be a person of character.

"Is character an important quality for your child to develop? Yes, if you want the best for your child. Yes, if you expect the other results on your list to manifest themselves to the highest levels.

"You see, my friends, *true* character is that rare quality able to raise mere, mortal man from ordinary circumstance to greatness. A person of integrity, trustworthy and reliable, is prepared and capable of performing the task for which he was created, but it takes character to speak up, step out, and perform that task."

Our small group was in a good place. We were mentally locked into the old man as he continued to make connections that, while they were fairly simple and obviously true, we had never read about or heard explained in that way. As we listened, and in my case furiously wrote down everything he said, Jones remained on the pier deck in front of us, sitting cross-legged and comfortable.

"I think your list is good," Jones said at one point. "Twenty-one is a good number, but how does a parent cover that much ground? At some level everyone understands that good parenting is just life coaching at a high and very critical level.

"Most parents try to impress upon their children that where they end up in life has something to do with the decisions they make. Easy examples would be the decisions made about where a person receives an education or how much of an education . . . or *what kind* of an education . . . or if they get an education at all.

"There are decisions about who to marry and when to get married or whether to get married.

"Folks make decisions about money and saving and debt. Where to live? Rent? Buy? There are decisions about whether or not to borrow money. And how much to borrow, as much as is needed or as much as one can get? If one doesn't have the money now, should a purchase be made at all? There are decisions about monthly payments and what should be paid down. Does a person expect to make payments for ten years? Never? Forever? What about credit cards?"

Jones stood up and walked slowly in front of us as he thought out loud. "A big one? A little one? You have to make the decision now, today. Why not two and both of them medium-sized? Fast or slow? Tomorrow the facts will have changed, so what will it be? How much? Red or white? Now? Later? New? Used? How used? There are many decisions to make, and every one of them moves a person to a slightly different position on life's chessboard."

The old man stopped pacing and faced us. "For most people there is no percentage of time and effort in an adult life that has more effect on every other part of life than what one does for a living. That's business. Whether one has a job, owns a little store or a big factory, or manages a place for someone else, it's all business."

Jones's blue eyes narrowed slightly as he deconstructed the puzzle in a way that we could put the pieces to use in our lives. I could see the wheels turning in the old man's head. "No matter what the business . . . or how one is involved," Jones said carefully, "do you all agree that the decisions a person makes on a daily basis have great impact on that business and his value to that business?"

We looked at each other quickly before nodding. That seemed to be an easy yes. We all agreed.

"So a person's long-term level of success or failure—as an employee, a manager, or an owner—in any part of business will be greatly determined by the quality and accuracy of his or her decisions. Decisions really matter? Is that what you're saying?"

Again, we agreed. Yes. Decisions absolutely do matter. They matter in the short and long term.

"We're coming up on an unavoidable connection between business and parenting," Jones said. "Stay with me here. Every decision you ever made—the best ones and the worst ones—were, at their base, merely a product of your thinking at that time. It is one's thinking that governs the decisions one makes every day.

"Decisions about what to do and how to do it become one's actions.

"Actions produce results of one kind or another, and those results are seen by everyone.

"Over time those actions and their results work in tandem to create what we call a reputation . . ."

Jones paused and then said, "Think about your list of results. That list, were it presented as an inventory of what a person had become—a catalog of one person's results—would reflect a substantial reputation. But what was the root, the beginning, of that powerful reputation? What had to be established first, long ago, in order that the pieces to life's puzzle might obediently move into place through the years?"

"The thinking," several of us said aloud.

"Yes, the essence of one's thinking," Jones said, "shows up in business. One's thought process is akin to a single seed, sprouting into a plant, growing for years, and finally bearing its fruit in adulthood. The quality of that fruit—now sweet or bitter—was determined long ago by how the plant was cared for in its early stages of development.

"This is why parenting our children is so important. Childhood is quite simply the easiest time to shape critical thinking. Many schools today have given themselves over to teaching students *what* to think. Ironically, that is a perfect example of bad thinking. But, of course, as a society we possess an incredible ability to think logically to wrong—and sometimes dangerous—conclusions.

"*What* a person thinks is determined by *how* a person thinks.

This is true whether the conclusion at which a person arrives is accurate, safe, and profitable—or stupid, vicious, and liable to bankrupt the company.

"Yes . . ." Jones looked up and nodded as if confirming what he was saying to himself. "*What* a person thinks is absolutely and always determined by *how* a person thinks. This is why, as parents, you must be on guard against those who would teach your children *what* to think and why you must be on the front lines of teaching your children *how* to think."

Jones stopped talking and looked at the bay. I tried to see what might have gotten his attention, but it all seemed the same to me. I glanced at my watch and saw that it was eight o'clock. Sure enough, the old man said, "That's all for this evening." Turning back to us, he asked, "Next week?"

"Yes," we all answered. "Please."

Jones smiled. And with that, he nodded, flashed a wave, and was gone.

Eleven

B aker Larson climbed the huge, winding staircase, crossed the broad veranda, and rang the doorbell. He had done harder things in his life, but for some reason pushing the button to the right of the massive double doors made his knees weak. *This is crazy*, he thought as he waited.

The evening before, Baker had run into the old man again, and this time Sealy had been there too. In reality, the couple hadn't "run into him" so much as they had walked outside to find the old man standing there as if he were waiting for them. Not having completely moved into their apartment, Baker had no idea how the old man found them, but there he was, leaning against their newly acquired, extremely used car Sealy had helped him pick out the day before.

Baker had talked to his wife about the old man incessantly since that morning in the wheat field. He had talked to Jones several times and was excited for Sealy to finally meet him. The doubtful expression on her face every time he brought up the subject of Jones bothered him. It was as if she suspected him of making up the whole thing. Because of that, Baker had purposely left out the part about the bird in the old man's pocket.

Maybe nobody's home, Baker thought, hoping for that to be the case despite the forty or so cars jammed into the driveway. *Some kind of party,* he decided as he rang the doorbell a second time. *Well, maybe there are so many folks that they can't hear the bell.* He was grasping at straws and knew it.

This unannounced visit had been Jones's idea. Or his plan or whatever it was. In any case, the old man had fixed him with those eyes and said to do this. So here he was.

Baker knew the guy he was supposed to see. At least, Baker knew *of* him, but then so did everyone else around Mobile and Baldwin County. The man owned car dealerships, restaurants, and a real estate company with offices scattered throughout several states. He was financially diversified in a way that was beyond Baker's ability to fathom.

Baker looked at the expansive porch and the immaculately groomed front yard. The house itself was enormous. Baker had seen big houses before, but this place was different somehow. It was not flamboyant or pretentious. It was just huge. For some reason he had never really thought about, Baker had always harbored a prejudice or resentment toward people who lived in homes like this, but he had heard nothing but good things about Jack Bailey. Still, Baker was nervous.

Worst of all, he didn't know *why* he was nervous. Maybe because he thought he might be jealous of this man he didn't even know. Perhaps, Baker thought, he was interrupting a party. Surely all those cars were not owned by the Baileys.

Baker had never been the anxious type, but he knew that the way he felt lately had a lot to do with his own financial situation. It had not been too long ago that he could have made a long list of reasons why he was broke, but the old man had shifted his thinking with one simple conversation. "If your situation is the fault of anything or anyone else," Jones had told him, "there is very little hope and absolutely zero power over your own life.

"Responsibility is about hope and control. And, Baker," Jones asked, "who doesn't want hope for a greater future that their choices control? You have been granted free will, son. You just didn't know it. At this very moment you are beginning a brand-new race. Now is the time for you to seek wisdom like you would look for a lost child or buried treasure. Don't be like average people. Most folks look for their car keys with more energy than they search for the wisdom that can change their lives.

"The power wrapped up in the principle of responsibility is unleashed by correct thinking. Consider this statement: 'I have had some crazy and tragic things happen in my life, and I couldn't control any of them. But in response to those crazy and tragic things, I have made choices that have taken me down a path to a place I do not like.'

"Son, if you can understand and believe that, it will be a defining moment in your journey. Do you see, Baker? If you can understand and believe that you have made choices that took you to a place you *don't* like, doesn't it just make logical sense that you can now make choices that will take you to a place you *do* like? Yes. Of course it does."

Jones patted Baker on the back and added, "So now your game becomes one of seeking wisdom and harnessing the power of that wisdom in order to make better choices."

The old man was right, Baker knew, and he now had a firm grip on that concept. With that shift in his thinking came hope for the future and a certainty that he and his family could . . . no . . . Baker had a certainty that he and his family *would* weather this storm. Exactly how that would be accomplished, he was not yet sure.

Baker did not ring the doorbell again and had turned to leave when the door opened. A tall, bald-headed man stepped out onto the huge front porch with a friendly smile. He appeared to be in his early sixties and was trim and fit. "How're you doing?" the man said as he approached with his hand out.

"Ah . . . fine," Baker said as he shook hands. "Yes, fine. Thanks."

Baker paused a beat too long, and sensing his uncertainty, the man quickly filled what might have turned into an awkward silence. He smiled and motioned Baker toward the entrance. "We're glad you're here. Man, I'm sorry it took so long to get to the door. I didn't even hear the bell ring. Come on through the house with me. Everyone is out by the pool or on the wharf."

Before the man could reach the doorway, however, Baker spoke up. "Sir, I am embarrassed to say this . . ." The man turned. "Sir, I wasn't invited to your gathering, and I know I'm intruding . . ."

No longer smiling broadly but still with a pleasant and welcoming expression on his face, the man said, "Oh, okay. Well, no problem. Can I help you with something?"

Baker looked at the ground briefly before taking a breath and saying, "Honestly, I'm not sure. Probably not . . . ah . . . as I said, I wasn't invited to your party . . . um . . . I was kind of *told* to be here. I was told to see you."

The man was several inches taller than Baker and aware of the younger man's uneasiness. Baker didn't seem threatening to him or even strange, just extremely uncomfortable. The man moved a couple of paces around Baker and went down one step of the staircase. There, he leaned against the teak banister. It didn't register with Baker until later, but the tall man had placed himself in a lower position, physically. And he had done it purposely so as not to further intimidate the already nervous younger man before him.

"You were *told* to see me? Okay. That sounds like a story."

"That's really all I know. Jones just told me to see you. I probably shouldn't have come, and I'm sorry if—"

Jack held his hand up, asking for silence without saying so. "Jones?" he asked simply.

"Yes sir."

"White hair? Blue eyes? Jeans and a T-shirt?"

"Yes sir."

Jack shook his head and looked away from Baker. To himself, he said aloud, "So he's still alive."

Baker heard the softly spoken words and responded. "Yes sir. He is. He is alive. Though I almost shot him a while back."

Jack's eyebrows flew up. "You what?"

Baker shrugged it off with a chuckle and a shake of his head. "Nothing, really. It's a long story. He just crossed my path on the worst day of my life. Kind of surprised me is all."

Jack nodded. Dryly, he said, "Yeah, he has a way of showing up like that." Jack stuck out his hand. "I'm Jack Bailey. Please, tell me your name again."

"I'm Baker Larson, Mr. Bailey," he answered, shaking Jack's hand for the second time. "It's nice to meet you. I am sorry to interrupt, but he did tell me to be here."

"Call me Jack, please. If you call me Mr. Bailey, I'll be looking around for my father." It was a line Jack used often. It relaxed people and made them smile. "So, Baker, what about our friend?" Jack asked, eager for information. "Is he still around?"

"As far as I know . . . well, yes. I'm sure he is. My wife and I are meeting him again next Thursday evening."

Jack stopped for a moment. He knew there was no sense in trying to find him. If the old man had wanted, he would have come with Baker. *This guy,* Jack thought as he looked at the younger man, *is my key to seeing the old man again. But why is he here? And what am I supposed to do?*

"Well now," Jack said, "you are not interrupting at all. In fact, I insist you stay. We've fired up the grills and are just eating, talking, and letting the kids play in the water."

"If you're sure," Baker said.

"I am. You hungry?" Jack was moving down the steps and motioned for the younger man to follow.

Baker smiled and did so. "I'm always hungry," he answered. "But first . . . you obviously know the old man. And he told you to just call him Jones as well?"

Already halfway across the front yard, Jack stopped and smiled. "Yes, I called him Jones. Just Jones. I knew some guys a long time ago, though, who called him Garcia. Some called him Chen. Jones to me, though."

Baker looked intrigued. "A long time ago?"

"Yes, twenty-eight years ago, in fact. I haven't seen him since."

"You're kidding!" Baker exclaimed.

Jack came out of his thoughts back to the present. "Come on around back. Let's get some food. I can already tell that we have a lot to talk about."

When Baker got his first look at the back of the house, he was flabbergasted. He had never seen anything to compare with what lay before him.

"What do you reckon, Baker?" Jack said. "Me? I figure there's about a million kids here."

The children were not what Baker had seen first, but he had to agree. Truly there were kids everywhere. They were on the slide, in the pool, jumping off the wharf into the bay, lining up to ride water toys pulled by the boats, and eating hamburgers and barbecue and pizzas. There were plenty of adults too. By the way they watched the kids, Baker could tell immediately they were mostly parents. "Who are these folks?" he asked Jack. "Do you do this every Saturday afternoon?"

"It seems like it sometimes," Jack said. "I know our neighbors probably think so. But this particular group of boys and girls are fishing buddies of mine." Baker waited for the explanation that comment promised, and Jack obliged. "A lot of these children are sick. The ones who aren't sick are friends of the kids who are. At a fund-raising event awhile back, I announced from the stage that I would take all of these kids fishing if the audience raised a certain amount of money. They did, and I'm still doing it. This was just a day right in the middle of the trips. Mary Chandler, my wife, figured to get them all together at once and let 'em have some more fun."

"You have got to be kidding!" Baker exclaimed. "You're taking *all* these kids fishing?"

"Yep. It's taking a while, and I'm whipped, but it's been awesome. For me as well as for them. We've only had a few postponed trips because of bad weather, so I've been out a lot."

Jack changed the subject. "You said you were hungry. Let's eat."

Beyond the pool with a view of the bay was what Baker could only describe as an outdoor kitchen. Lounge chairs, a stainless sink, a refrigerator, a freezer . . . but the thing that caught Baker's eye was the cooking station that wrapped around the kitchen in a semicircle. At least twenty-five feet in length, it was covered in polished stone and inset with six Kamado Joe ceramic grills. "Oh my gosh!" Baker was unable to hide his excitement. "You have the Kamado Joes! Good grief . . . there're six of them! Oh man! Wow! Two Classics, two BigJoes, and two stainless-steel ProJoes. Wow!"

Baker knew what he was looking at. The Kamado Joe is a

domed-style cooker created with a special ceramic, giving it an unusual ability to insulate. It uses natural lump charcoal—no chemicals, even when lighting—and the temperature can be controlled in small increments from 225 all the way to 750 degrees. "Man," Baker said to Jack, "I like your house, and the pool is great, but this is my deal. Man! I'm in chef's heaven!"

Jack laughed and said, "Great, I'm glad you like the kitchen. Here, eat," he added, shoving a plate at Baker. "They're doing pizzas on the two at the far end. Grilled vegetables on the next one in line, two twenty-pound turkeys on number four, burgers and dogs on five, and fourteen racks of ribs—going fast it looks like—on the Kamado Joe closest to us."

Baker liked to cook and loved to cook outdoors. Several years before, thinking he would save some money, he had purchased one of the cheaper knockoffs being imported to compete with the Kamado Joe. Within six months the finish had faded, and the spring hardware and handle had rusted; and several months after that, the ceramic (or whatever it was) began to crack and crumble.

Baker went online and checked out Kamado Joe. After reading all the ecstatic reviews, he paid only a little more than he had for the knockoff, cooked on it that night, and started what Sealy called "Baker's love affair with the Kamado Joe."

Now, in the presence of six Kamado Joe grills, it was almost more than Baker could take. He got some of everything, including more pizza than he would have had Sealy been there, but the lure of wood-fire flavor pepperoni was much too strong. Jack loaded up, too, and while balancing plates on his arms, motioned to Baker with his head. "Let's spread out over here."

They stopped at a table on the edge of the property. After a few minutes of small talk about the taste of this or that and a short but passionate speech by Baker listing the many reasons

Kamado Joes "had it all over" gas grills, Jack got down to the real subject on their minds.

"Baker," he started, "I don't know how you ran into that old man, but I think it tells me something about your current situation. And now you've talked with him a few times?"

"Yes sir. I have."

Jack smiled and nodded. "Good. Well, if you have a brain in your head—which I can plainly see that you do—that tells me something about your future." Jack ate some of the smoked turkey between two slices of bread and was silent for a bit. He looked out over the bay, watching the kids on a big banana-shaped float being pulled by a large ski boat.

Jack took a breath to speak, but Baker beat him to it. "Why am I here today?"

Jack's mouth closed. He thought for a beat before countering, "That's what I was going to ask. Why *are* you here? Don't get me wrong . . . I'm glad that you are. But if Jones is behind it, there's a reason. What am I supposed to tell you? What are you here to see? Or is it something you are to teach me?"

"I doubt that," Baker said and took the last bite of pizza.

Jack cocked his head. "Really? If you seriously doubt there is anything I could learn from you, then maybe you haven't been around the old man as much as I thought." Baker's head pulled back. "Kidding," Jack said and punched Baker playfully on the shoulder. "Just kidding. Look, Baker, you and I both know that whatever it is we are supposed to do or find out, it's probably right in front of us."

"Perspective," Baker said.

"Yep," Jack agreed. "Perspective. So let's explore every angle of the puzzle."

"Do you know what the puzzle is?" Baker asked.

"I do not, but I know that Jones would say to persist without exception." Jack collected his thoughts while gathering their napkins, cups, and the remnants of the meal. He moved to a nearby trash can and dumped the paper plates before continuing. Settling again at the table, he said, "As a deeper lesson about persistence, Jones convinced me long ago that most folks greet confusion with surrender. Most people, when they don't know what to do, do nothing. The average person meets an obstacle and tells himself, 'This is not for me,' or 'I am not the kind of person who does things like this.' Average people respond to confusion in an average way. They stop. But people who achieve extraordinary results think differently. They understand something very significant about confusion."

"What would that be?" Baker asked.

"'Confusion precedes learning,'" Jack said. "That is a direct quote from the old man. Listen: confusion precedes learning. The anxious thoughts that seem so puzzling or discouraging are actually your very gateway to understanding. Only by persistently doing battle with the things you cannot *yet* do or that which you do not *yet* understand can you ever hope to achieve what average people never accomplish."

"The 'yet' part is the key, right?" Baker remarked.

"Yes," Jack agreed, "it is. When confronted with a difficult task, most people concede, at least to themselves, 'I can't do that.' The distinction provided by the knowledge that confusion always precedes learning is 'I can't do that *yet*.' When a person understands the concept, it opens wide the possibility of an entirely different life than the one presently lived."

Baker thought about that and then said, "Slow down and explain this. I'm not trying to be funny, but I'm a bit confused right now. I do think, though—when I understand this completely, the concept will change my life."

Jack laughed and nodded. "It absolutely will," he said.

"Okay, stay with me. A sign of a person's maturity is his ability to live with—even *in*—confusion. The average person meets the edge of confusion and turns away. He runs from confusion at its beginning, at its first appearance. 'I can't do this,' he says. 'This is not for me.' He will not live with or even near confusion and seeks an easier path.

"The mature person—the high achiever—will understand that life's grand prizes are guarded by confusion. The mature person senses the victory that exists beyond confusion and says, 'I cannot do this . . . *yet*. I am not good at this *yet*, but I will work and learn and become better until I am competent, then excellent, then great! I will struggle and persist through confusion until I break through to the understanding or greater skill required for victory.'

"'I cannot play the guitar . . . yet.' 'I cannot do this algebra problem . . . yet.' 'I am not good at public speaking . . . yet.' Do you see?"

"I do," Baker answered. "It's a thought process, right? It opens up new possibilities for almost everything. Anything a person might want to become—a great parent, a successful sales executive, a fast reader—everything is within reach. When you think about it, it's a mind-set based on reality. Why would anyone think they would be great right out of the box? I want to be a great cook. I am not a great cook . . . yet. Therefore, I will live with the confusion and disappointment of ruined meals as I practice until I master the skills and timing I need to be a great cook."

Baker thought for a moment, wanting to understand clearly and form the idea into words he could remember. "It is amazing," he said finally. "The whole concept of 'confusion before learning' means that confusion guards the answers we seek."

Jack was quiet, nodding as Baker continued the thought. "I've got to be willing to enter into and do battle with the confusion in order to reach the victory on the other side. It's like, I am here, confusion is in front of me, and just beyond confusion waits the answer or skill I need to take my life in a new and incredible direction."

Suddenly Baker's eyes opened wide, and he looked at Jack as if he had just reached the other side on this very issue. "It's simple, really," he said, "and incredibly ordinary when you think about it. Why are we so afraid of confusion? Confusion is nothing but a word for 'not knowing the answer.' And really, isn't it true that every time, right before we know the answer, we always . . . don't know the answer!" Baker laughed in amazement and relief. "When I think of it like that, I am ready to deal with confusion and be a lot calmer—and happier—in the process!"

The two men were quiet for a time. Baker continued to concentrate greatly as he arranged the new thoughts on the "permanent" shelf in his mind. Jack understood what was taking place and patiently allowed the younger man time to cognitively cement his newfound perspective. He was keenly aware of the vast difference in achievement levels demonstrated by those who understood this principle versus those who did not.

"You know," Jack said when the time seemed right, "I haven't seen Jones in twenty-eight years." Baker nodded, though neither man looked at the other. "I obviously have *known* that he was gone." Jack furrowed his brow, concentrating intently as if a specific thought was out of focus and just beyond his reach.

He took a drink from the glass and rattled the ice. "I have been tossing around that idea since you showed up. Kind of like a cat would play with a string, you know? I've known he was gone, but I never *felt* like he was gone. It's like he's been gone in my head but still here in my heart . . . It doesn't make sense really. Even to me. But I still feel that way." Jack looked over at Baker. "I mean, right now, I still feel that way."

Again they sat quietly, Baker consumed with thoughts of the future, Jack having been gripped suddenly by the past. Jack Bailey and Baker Larson were very different from each other but united somehow by an old man who had touched both their lives.

Finally Jack turned to face the younger man. "Tell me your story, Baker," he said. "Tell me about your family. What do you do? Where are you from? When did Jones show up exactly? What does the future hold for Baker Larson? I want to hear it all."

For a long time Baker told him just that. He answered every question Jack asked, and with only a little prompting, Baker explained exactly where he was financially and the hope he had gained lately because of Jones. That hope, he confessed, did not seem based in reality, but it was there, deep within him, just the same.

Baker told the story of the wheat field and every detail he could remember about that day, with only three minor exceptions. Jack listened to Baker describe how the old man had appeared with the starlings that morning and how Jones had taken the gun from him and how he seemed compelled to stay and listen. He told Jack everything he could remember that Jones had said.

Baker left out the part about killing the birds because he was afraid of what Jack's reaction might be. Neither did he say anything about the old man touching the underside of the starling's wing. Baker had worked that moment over in his mind more than a few times and couldn't explain it, not even to himself. So how could he possibly say to someone he just met, "I saw a guy touch a bird and the black feathers turned white?" Ah . . . no. He couldn't tell anyone that story. That tale, Baker knew, would only make folks think *he* was strange.

The last thing Baker skipped was the part about the old man putting the bird in his pocket. By now he loved Jones and knew Jack felt the same way. The whole putting-a-dead-bird-in-your-pocket thing felt too awkward. Baker thought it might make the old man seem senile or something. In any case, it was unnecessary to the larger story, so he kept it to himself.

When he finished, Jack had a couple of questions. "Where is your family living now, Baker?"

"We're in an apartment," he answered. "It's a room for us and a room for the girls. Nothing fancy, but it's fine. I was embarrassed at first. Now, I just want to figure out some stuff and get rolling in the right direction."

"How are you set for vehicles?"

Baker rolled his head over and smiled. "Well, the two pretty ones we had, I took 'em back to *your* place." Jack winced, and Baker laughed. "Oh well, don't feel bad. I don't. Your guys at the dealership got us in something used—*pre-owned*, I think was the term they preferred—and we are good. Hey, I can actually afford these."

"I don't mean to be nosy, but if you don't have your land anymore and the land was your source of income . . . and you don't have a job yet . . ."

"How'd I get the money for the cars?"

Jack lifted his chin and smiled. "Just curious."

Baker shrugged. "Man, you have no idea how much stuff we had in that house. Trust me, it was a lot. We had a few days to get out, and it was one massive yard sale until we left. We sold almost everything. Three televisions, several cameras, a pair of binoculars, two sets of golf clubs . . . We didn't need all that in an apartment." After a pause, he added, "Truthfully, we didn't need all that stuff at all."

Baker brightened. "You know, what's great is that Sealy is good with everything we're doing. It was hard at first . . . okay, actually, it's still hard, but we're toughing it out. We're living indoors, right? There are folks who aren't."

"That's true," Jack said. "That is a well-chosen perspective."

"Yeah, Jones told me that," Baker said. "I keep saying it, you know . . . the part about living indoors? I need to remember that. I feel better when I do."

Jack agreed. "That is a human absolute. We all feel better when we are grateful. There is great wisdom in understanding that no matter the situation, there is always something for which we can choose to be grateful."

Baker thought about that and commented, "That's true. It never occurred to me that when I am grateful, I have chosen to think that way. That is a new one . . . that I can choose to . . ." Baker's eyes brightened. "Hey, that *is* perspective, right? Perspective is, ultimately, how I *choose* to see a situation." He reached over and playfully slapped Jack on the leg with the back of his hand. "Here is something I am grateful for . . . I did not have to sell my Kamado Joe!"

Jack laughed. "So you have one too? No wonder you know so much about them."

"Mine isn't the BigJoe, though. It's the Classic. I told Sealy if worst comes to worst, we might be living outside, but we *will* be eating well."

"That's it," a voice said, and the two men turned to see Jones smiling and slowly clapping his hands in applause only several feet away. "I think he's got it," the old man said. "What do you think, Jack?"

Twelve

J ones!" Baker exclaimed. "Where did you come from?"

Jack didn't say a word but stood and went straight to the old man, wrapping him in a bear hug. "I can't believe it's you," he said.

Jones delivered a hug of his own before struggling to escape the arms of the much larger man. "It's not going to be me if you squish me like a bug," he laughed.

Baker got up from the table and stood to the side with a grin on his face, watching the reunion. Jack finally released his old friend and wiped tears from his face.

Jack put his hands on his hips, suddenly striking a mock-serious pose. "Do you know how long you've been gone?"

The old man's white eyebrows went up. "Do you?"

"Yes," Jack answered. "You've been gone more than twenty-eight years."

"Hm . . . seems like yesterday to me." Jones moved to the water's edge and motioned for the men to follow. "And any-way, I haven't really been gone. I've been around." Jack opened his mouth to comment, but before he could get a word out, Jones spoke again. "This place is beautiful, son. You've worked diligently . . . wisely." He waved an arm at the crowd of people, mostly children, and added, "I'm proud of how you are using the rewards of your success as well."

Once more, Jack was about to speak when, again, Jones spoke first. Lifting his arms as if to encompass the entire property with all the children and their parents, he said, "It was your efforts years ago that made all the parts of this day possible. You worked in faith. You labored on through confusion, around despair, above distractions, and occasionally under attack. You did the work with a song in your heart and a smile on your face. You did this even when you did not feel like singing or smiling or even going outside to face another day."

Jones put his hand on Baker and briefly squeezed his arm. Nodding toward Jack, he said, "This man knows the uncertainty you are facing right now. He has been through the fire—several times, in fact—and the Jack Bailey you see now is a product of that fire. He has allowed himself to be molded and shaped. Jack's life seed—which he planted intentionally and tended carefully—is now producing the fruit he expected as the just reward of obeying principles and doing the required work."

Jones's blue eyes carefully searched the yard. When he found the person he was looking for, the old man smiled and pointed. "The tall girl in green . . . long blonde hair . . . she's pushing the two children in the swing. Do you see her?" Both men responded affirmatively.

"Her name is Bella. Bella Serra. Beautiful name, isn't it?" Jones asked. After the men agreed, he said, "Yes. It's a beautiful name for a beautiful young girl. She is not sick. Neither does she have a close friend who is ill. Bella has a heart to help those who are hurting . . . those who are less fortunate. And she's not the only one," he said to Baker. "There're quite a few folks—young and old—who have been inspired by Jack and Mary Chandler."

Jones placed a hand on Jack's shoulder. "Yes sir," he said to the much taller man, "I am proud of your influence and example."

"Speaking of Mary Chandler, here she comes," Jack said. "I'll warn you in advance, Baker, she can get bossy at times like this."

Jones laughed at the comment. Baker, attempting to hide his grin, asked, "Times like what?" The three men were on the edge of the wharf, facing the house, and Mary Chandler had just walked out the door.

"Times like this: cleanup time." Jack paused, and they watched his wife hurry down the back steps. "She's beautiful," he went on, never taking his eyes from her, "but when there's work to be done, especially out here, she is in full event mode, so look out!" They all laughed out loud as they watched her walk toward them with purpose.

The party was over. There was still an hour or so of daylight left and a lot to hose down, mop up, and put away. Mary Chandler was rounding the pool with an eye on her husband and his guest, whom she had met earlier. Her jaw dropped, her face brightened, and she actually picked up speed when she recognized Jones.

Sure enough, Mary Chandler had a long list of things that needed to be done right then, and she was not shy about including Baker in the detail. Of course, he had been happy to help and appreciated the opportunity to spend even more time with Jack.

Jones, as it turned out, had not been asked to do any work at all. Mary Chandler had whisked him away to sit on the back porch, declaring that for once, she wanted the old man to herself. For the next several hours, every time Jack looked their way, his old friend was deep in conversation with his wife.

Jones sipped his iced tea and watched the graceful woman closely. She was right in front of him, seated on the couch with its back to the water in order that her guest might enjoy the view. Jones was not really interested, however, so at that moment, as spectacular as it was, the view was going unappreciated. He was with this woman at this time for a specific reason, and that reason had nothing to do with whether or not he enjoyed gazing at the bay.

That reason, when he had broached the subject seconds before, had totally shut down the previous, engaging conversation. Mary Chandler Bailey was no longer smiling and holding his eyes with her own. She was no longer the polished hostess. Instead, she looked to the side, down and away, avoiding his question and now, apparently, him as well.

Years ago the old man had spent his time almost exclusively with Jack and had met Mary Chandler on only a couple of occasions. Incredibly, however, after almost three decades away the old man seemed to know the woman almost as well as he did her husband. He referenced places and people she knew, and she was amazed, enjoying every word. Until he brought up the one thing she did not wish to discuss.

Mary Chandler had grown up in a middle-class home as the only child of two loving parents. Her father was an outdoorsman and taught his daughter to shoot and to ride and to fish. She dearly loved her father, but it was her mother who was her very best friend. Mary Chandler remained best friends with her mother during her teen years and on through college. Even after she and Jack were married, Mary Chandler very much enjoyed her mother's company and welcomed her advice.

It was after the children came that some sort of distance between them became evident. Mary Chandler was never quite sure why she felt the way she did, but the resentment was real. *Don't tell me again how you would do it*, she often thought while looking directly at her mother. But outward respect for older people—especially her parents—was deeply ingrained in Mary

Chandler, so she remained silent, never giving voice to any of her irritations.

Not talking about the disconnect only widened the gulf between the two women over time. Mary Chandler didn't say anything because she didn't understand why she felt the way she did and wanted to avoid an argument. Her mother didn't say anything because she loved her daughter greatly and was worried that any conversation about whatever was happening would make it worse.

So it happened that for years, the two had allowed a festering unknown to create distance between a mother and daughter who loved one another. Their relationship was never horrible; it just wasn't what it had once been. And now Mary Chandler often reminded herself, it was too late. The conversations with her mother were over. She would never have another.

"Mary Chandler," Jones had asked, "how do you think your mother is doing?"

"Not well at all," she had answered and pursed her lips. As she broke eye contact with the guest with whom she had been thrilled to engage only seconds before, Mary Chandler unconsciously crossed her arms, then her legs.

"I don't mean to intrude," Jones said, "but I'd really like to know. How do you think she is?"

Mary Chandler rolled her head back toward the old man and looked at him over her reading glasses. "Jones," she said in a suddenly weary voice, "I have heard Jack talk about you for almost three decades. If I have learned one thing about you during that time, it is that, yes, you do mean to intrude. No offense, you understand. Of all people, I am grateful for your intrusion into our lives years ago. But this is different. Not even you can give my mother perspective about anything anymore. So please . . . please . . . I don't want to talk about it. Okay?"

Taking a deep breath, Mary Chandler looked out at the

wharf and saw that Jack was still there before turning back to Jones. "Thank you," she said.

"For what?" the old man asked.

Her eyebrows lifted in mild surprise. "For not talking about my mother."

"Ah, yes," Jones said pleasantly. "So, Mary Chandler . . . how do you think your mother is doing?"

"Not . . . well . . . at all," Mary Chandler said through clenched teeth. "Why are you doing this? What's the point? What do you want me to say? She's alive, but not really . . ."

Jones saw the tears tracking down the beautiful face of the middle-aged woman and said, "It's okay. I'm your friend. I am also a friend of your mother's."

With that, Mary Chandler's head jerked up. "What?" she said incredulously. "You know my mother?"

"Of course," he shrugged. "I'm old. I've been in and out of Mississippi for years. I know a lot of folks."

"But my mother?"

"Yep. I know your mother," Jones said. "And, frankly, I know how she is doing. I just wanted to know how *you* thought she was doing."

"Well, I told you."

"Yes, you did," the old man said. "May I ask why you are so angry about her situation?"

Mary Chandler's jaw dropped. "Have you seen her?"

"Yes."

"Then you don't need to ask that question. My mother is dead—except that she is not. Alzheimer's has completely shut down her brain. For two years it got worse and worse. Now she doesn't even talk anymore. She eats, sleeps, and goes to the bathroom. That's it."

Mary Chandler was quiet for a moment, and Jones didn't

say anything either. He waited, knowing she had more to say. "What my mother is experiencing is cruel and unusual punishment," she continued. "There is no reason for her to live. There is no purpose in this. Yet the doctors say that she is strong and well physically. Why? This is wrong. It should not be allowed to happen. God is not paying attention."

"Why do you think that?" he asked.

"Because if God were paying attention, He would allow my mother to die . . . to pass away peacefully. As I said, my mother can no longer serve a purpose, and without purpose what she is experiencing is absolutely meaningless, unnecessary, and, yes, cruel."

Jones leaned forward. "I'm curious," he said. "Can you not think of a single purpose for your mother's continued life on this earth?"

Without hesitation and barely disguising her increasing annoyance, Mary Chandler bluntly declared, "None."

Jones sat back with a sigh. "Another discouraged seller of shoes, I see. Well," he said as he slapped his hands on his thighs, "I've dealt with a lot of them. No worries. Let's get to it."

Mary Chandler frowned. "Get to what? And you said I am a what? A seller of shoes? What does that mean?"

Smiling, Jones said, "We are going to get to a place of proper perspective. And what I said was that you were a discouraged seller of shoes. It's just my own little inside joke. It's my way of referring to folks who base their conclusions on a single view from the wrong side of a situation. Tragically, it usually shuts them down completely. But in your case, it's tragic and ironic."

Mary Chandler did not smile or even move her head. "At the risk of becoming more offensive," she said tersely, "why don't you just explain the discouraged seller of shoes thing?"

"All right," Jones responded. "A hundred years ago two shoe companies each sent a salesman to Africa. They traveled on the same ship and arrived at their destination at the same time. Within twenty-four hours, however, the first salesman was composing a telegram for his boss, declaring the company's expansion into Africa to be a disaster of epic proportions. 'Stop all increased production!' the salesman wrote. "No one here wears shoes!'

"At the same time the other salesman was also composing a telegram for his boss. 'Send more salesmen,' he wrote, 'and push the factory to twenty-four-hour production. We have hit the jackpot. No one here wears shoes!'"

Jones cocked his head, waiting to see if Mary Chandler understood the point of his story.

"So you are saying there is something I do not see," she stated carefully. "Tell me, please."

"Do you understand the reality of what is known as the butterfly effect?" he asked.

Mary Chandler frowned briefly. "Yes," she said. "I think I do. The reality would be that a person's actions are akin to the flap of a butterfly's wings or a ripple in a pond. A person's actions always affect the life of someone else, who affects the life of someone else, and so on. The initial action continues to make a difference for generations to come, correct?"

"Yes," Jones nodded, "that is correct." Narrowing his eyes, he asked, "Mary Chandler . . . I consider you a wonderful person. You are a valuable wife, mother, mentor, and friend. Do you—or maybe I should ask *did* you—did you ever use anything your mother taught you?"

"What kind of question is that?" Mary Chandler answered. "Of course I did. And I still do. Every day. I use and pass on lessons my mother taught me about life. Every single day!"

"When did you decide you had learned enough?"

Mary Chandler stared at Jones. "I'm not sure I understand."

"Allow me to put it another way," Jones said. "When you

decided your mother's life was without purpose, you chose to forfeit the lessons she still had to teach."

"Jones," Mary Chandler said. "Allow *me* to say *this* again: she cannot understand anything. *Anything*, okay? My mother cannot understand anything!"

"Yes," Jones replied. "I'm beginning to think the condition runs in your family." As the meaning of that remark flew over Mary Chandler's head, he went on. "I'll explain it like this: As I've already stated, you are an incredible woman. Together, you and Jack have accomplished great things. You have helped many people. To this date, the effects of your butterfly wings on the lives of other people are many, long lasting, and ongoing. But there is more to be done. Much more . . .

"You see, my dear, there is a future that lies ahead of every man and woman. Our choices now—this week, this month, this year—are very sticky. Once made, their effects never go away. Rather, those choices about how we think and what we do are a constant presence. Every thought, every action is a choice, and even now the choices you have made in your life thus far are shifting and combining in order to create who you really are. Therefore, simple logic says that by paying careful attention to our choices from this point forward, we can create a future we choose instead of a future that 'happens.'

"In your case, Mary Chandler Bailey, you are a very accomplished human being. However, if you wish to have increased influence for good, if you desire greater financial options in order to give and help more, if you truly want to create hurricanes of opportunity for others with *your* butterfly wings, you must become the kind of person who can accomplish these things."

Mary Chandler was listening intently. Jones was about to close the circle on his narrative, and the truth of it would shock her. For a long time after she would wonder how she could have wasted so much time and energy because of what she referred to as her "eye condition." "I'll never know how much I missed," she liked to tell people. "I was blind as a bat—walking around all day, every day—never suspecting I could not see some things that were right in front of me."

"Amazingly," Jones finally said, "the very things you must master—to become the person you must become—in order to accomplish what lies ahead, are being taught by your mother right now, but you are not paying attention.

"For instance, to fulfill the purpose of your own life, you must learn greater patience and exhibit that patience publicly and privately. You must possess a greater spirit of gratefulness and effectively demonstrate greater appreciation to others for the purposes *they* are fulfilling. You must learn to forgive even when another does not reciprocate. You must also learn to accept forgiveness when it is offered and recognize that, sometimes, the offer is not verbalized but expressed in an action or from one's spirit.

"Your mother, Mary Chandler, is teaching these things right now. Today she is being used for a mighty purpose that will one day touch tens of thousands of lives through the life of her daughter . . . you. You are still her little girl, and she still loves you more than anything. She does not think in the same way you do anymore. But her soul—that spirit that was your mother—is *still* your mother."

Mary Chandler had begun to cry. Jones knelt on the porch's floor and took her hand. "Mary C?" he said quietly, causing her to look up, startled. Jones smiled and said, "Remember how many times she called you that when you were a little girl? Remember how it made you laugh? Years ago, in a conversation with Jack and me, you mentioned a song that she used to sing to you every night when she put you to bed. Do you remember it?"

With perfect pitch but faltering tone, Jones sang. As the tears flowed freely, Mary Chandler held on to the old man's hands with both of hers and pressed her head against his shoulder as his voice washed over her with memories from childhood.

> *Hush, my sweetheart. Close your eyes.*
> *It's almost time to say good night.*
> *No more worries; work is done.*
> *Sweet dreams now 'til morning sun.*

Jones lifted his shoulder, gently pulling it away, causing Mary Chandler to lift her head. As she looked into the old man's eyes, he squeezed her hands and asked, "Do you remember the rest?" She nodded. "Sing it with me," he said, "and tomorrow, go wrap your arms around your sweet mother . . . and sing the song for her."

Once more Jones sang the familiar tune, and with tears continuing to course down her cheeks, Mary Chandler joined her own voice with his. It was a moment that marked the beginning of what would become a greatly expanded level of searching, learning, and understanding for her. And there would be a renewed purpose, with direction and a trajectory in Mary Chandler's own life that she had never expected . . . or had even known was possible.

> *Hush, my sweetheart. Close your eyes.*
> *Now it's time to say good night.*
> *Daylight's fading; rest your bones.*
> *Don't be afraid; you're not alone.*

Mary Chandler held on tightly to the old man's hands until he got to his feet. With a squeeze, she released him and said, "Thank you. I don't know why I never saw that before."

Jones smiled and shrugged. "Well," he said softly, "now you

do." He shrugged again. "It's an old condition, a common story. I was blind, but now I see. Perspective changes everything." He motioned toward the empty end of the couch and said, "Looks like plenty of room to stretch out. Why don't you rest a bit? I'm sure Jack will be on up soon."

Suddenly Mary Chandler *was* tired. In fact, she was more exhausted than she could ever remember. With just the suggestion, she slowly lay down with barely the energy to get her feet up. Later she couldn't recall if she had even said good-bye. She remembered only her mother's song. Jones had placed his hand on her head while he softly sang it again, and by the time Jack woke her up to go inside, the old man was gone.

Thirteen

It was the Tuesday morning after I had seen him last at the Grand Hotel, and I drove to Fairhope to find the old man. I knew I would see him at the next parenting class, but I needed to see him sooner. I was not doing well. In fact, those were the exact words Polly had used that very morning. "You," my wife had declared with a finger pointed in my direction, "are not doing well."

It was true. I was not and did not need anyone to diagnose that fact for me. The book that was not being written was hanging over my days and mocking me with dreams at night. For some reason I was unable to concoct a good story. Matt was continuing to be patient and good humored—at least to my face—and I was grateful for his loyalty, but privately I had gone from concerned to alarmed to fearful. Now, it seemed, I had arrived at the level of disgust; and while it was all directed at myself, those closest to me endured a degree of grouchiness from me they did not deserve.

After walking the grounds of the Grand Hotel, through the marina, and scouring downtown Fairhope, I finally spotted Jones walking up the hill from the city pier. Quickly parking, I called after him and ran to catch up. He was waiting at the top of what was a much higher hill than I remembered.

I was already in a bad mood, and having run up Mount Kilimanjaro after a man who kept walking as I struggled up the cliff behind him did not soothe my irritation. Fortunately for him (and probably for me) I could not speak for several minutes. The lack of oxygen at that altitude prolonged my period of assimilation, which was a good thing. By the time I could breathe and talk, I had forgotten why I was aggravated in the first place.

"I've looked all over for you," was the first thing I said, to which Jones replied, "I haven't been all over. I've only been here and there."

"You know," I said to Jones, "when you're *out* of the area, I don't know where you are. And when you are *in* the area, I don't know where you are. Of course, you could be *in* the area, but because I don't know *when* or *if* I will see you again, it doesn't really matter that you are. That you are *in* the area, I mean. So you might as well, at least as far as I'm concerned, be out of the area."

Jones nodded seriously and said, "Fascinating. Would you write that down for me? I'd like to take it to a crazy person for translation."

After laughing at me about that, he headed toward the shade in a nearby front yard and sat down on the ground, motioning for me to join him.

"You're concerned about the book, ain't ya?" he said.

"Yes sir."

"No fantastic story?" he asked. "No spies? No war heroes? No folks traveling through time?"

I shook my head.

"Hm . . ." Jones put his hands behind his head and lay back in the grass. "How about a grave robber? You used a grave robber in *The Lost Choice*."

"No," I said. "I'm thinking 'grave robber' is not a character choice to trot out in more than one book."

He seemed to consider that thought before nodding. "You're probably right. Okay, no grave robbers. Looks like you are seriously stuck."

"Thanks for the encouragement."

"'Seriously stuck' isn't such a bad thing."

"Really?" I said drily.

"Really," Jones responded. 'Seriously stuck' provides a clearly defined opportunity. When one is seriously stuck, there is an obvious choice that must be made. You can do one of two things. You can quit, or you can break through to a new level of awareness and achievement. There ya go. Take your pick." He smiled contentedly and closed his eyes.

I waited to see if he would keep talking. When he did not, I shook my head and said, "When you say something like that, it seems very simple."

He did not open his eyes. In fact, the old man added a yawn to his sleepy posture as he responded. "It is simple. It ain't necessarily easy, but it is simple." Jones paused before continuing. "And," he said, "'seriously stuck' has another benefit. That condition is one of the few that allows the time needed to closely examine our surroundings. The answer one seeks when seriously stuck is never far away." He opened one eye to see if I was listening. Satisfied that I was, he closed it and settled into a more comfortable position.

"Well, I think I have looked close by for a story," I said, "but frankly there is nothing around here but a normal place with normal people doing normal things."

"What's wrong with that?" Jones inquired.

"Normal is just too ordinary," I tried to explain. "Normal is normal. People have to be entertained."

Jones furrowed his brow. "Are you trying to help folks change their lives or entertain 'em?"

"Both, I think. If the books don't entertain to a degree," I said, "people might not stick around long enough to be helped."

"You have a point there," he said. "Still, sometimes real life can be right entertaining. Keep an eye on it."

"I will," I promised.

Jones jumped to his feet. "Give me a ride?"

"Sure," I said. "Where to?"

"You just fetch the car," he said. "Baker Larson ought to be in town soon. Let's go see him."

I managed to get down the hill without injury and was on my way back up when I saw a guy who turned out to be Baker Larson walking across the front yard in which we had just been sitting to shake Jones's hand and give him a hug. I parked again—this time close by—and went to join them.

Baker and I were introduced, and Jones gave me a brief overview of their first encounter. Baker filled in a few blanks about their current situation, including the finances, and soon the three of us were sitting in the shade, just as Jones and I had done earlier. We talked about the heat and about fishing. We discussed ideas for a tree house in the oak that was above us and dissected the Atlanta Braves pitching staff before Jones abruptly changed the subject.

"Baker," he said, "you're looking to make a comeback, correct?"

"Yes sir. Absolutely," the younger man answered.

"So what is the biggest barrier to getting started on that comeback right away?"

"That's easy," Baker answered. "My credit is shot."

Uh-oh, I thought, swinging my eyes to Jones for the reaction. *He shouldn't have said that . . .*

"Hey, Baker . . ."

"Sir?"

"Read my mind." Jones bugged his eyes open and stuck his face toward the younger man.

Baker was puzzled but had enough experience with the old man to play along. "Ah, okay . . . ," he said and stared at Jones. Within seconds he had given up. "Oh well," he said, "I can't do it. So tell me . . . What are you thinking?"

Jones glanced at me and whistled. "Very nice," he said. "You hit it right on the nose. In fact, those were my very words: 'What are you thinking?'"

Baker frowned and said, "I don't get it."

Jones laughed. "That's exactly right. You're getting ahead of me, but that is correct. Say it again."

Baker lifted his hands in confusion. "I don't get it."

"Correct," Jones shot back playfully. "In this particular instance, you do not get it." Before the younger man could be offended, Jones explained. "Look, I'm just teasing, but to begin your comeback—no fooling around at all—you'll need to turn most of what you think . . . up . . . side . . . down. Do you hear me?"

Baker nodded grudgingly. "I hear you. Don't believe everything you think, right?"

"Correct. I'm glad you remember. What about the secret doctrine of extraordinary achievement—my little speech about not being like everyone else?"

"I got it," Baker said. "I say it to myself a lot."

"Good man," Jones nodded. "That just might be the best advice you ever get. It covers a lot of ground. So keep this in mind . . ." Jones was face to face with the younger man. "If you do *not* want an average life, you must be on guard against, and quietly suspicious of, conclusions made by conventional thinking."

"Like what?" Baker asked.

"Like your nonexistent credit at the present time," Jones said. "Conventional thinking says that is a bad thing."

"And you're about to tell me it's a good thing?" Baker said skeptically.

"It depends," Jones replied. "Do you want an average life or an extraordinary life?"

Baker said nothing. He simply stared at the old man.

"Son," Jones said, shifting and moving closer. "You have to answer that question for yourself. Average life . . . or extraordinary life? *You really do have to choose.*

"I know where you are right now. Don't try to hide your thinking. Examine it. Right now, you don't want to choose either one. You don't want to say anything. You figure that if you answer 'average,' then you're a loser for settling for less than the best for your family. On the other hand, you know that if you speak up and declare, 'I want to live an extraordinary life,' you've committed to do something different and *be* something different, and that is going to be tough. But you must *choose.*"

Jones gestured toward me. "Thirty some-odd years ago, I had much the same conversation with him. And his situation at that time makes you look like a king." Baker looked at me with more interest. "I told Andy the same thing you need to understand now . . . that if you do not choose, you'll end up like everyone else in the world who has never chosen. The people who do not actively choose a road to travel always default to the road everyone else is already on. They default to 'average.'

"So do you want to be different, Baker? Then choose. Most people would not. They *will* not. In fact, most people would leave right now, offended that anyone would dare talk to them this way. Most people in your place would probably hit me or cry or cuss.

"But you know what? I don't think you are 'most people.' I think you have 'extraordinary' running through your veins. You've just never known what to do about it. Well . . . I'm ready and willing to guide or assist you in any way I can, at least for a time. But first, you must choose." Jones eased back on his elbows, legs stretched out in front of him, but continued to watch the younger man carefully.

Baker paused only a moment before beginning to nod. Looking Jones in the eye, he said, "You're right. You are right about all that. And about me. I am scared. In fact, I don't know if I have ever been this scared. But maybe that's a good thing too. Even when I was a little boy getting picked on by the big kids, I always fought best when I was scared.

"I'm tired of doing things halfway. And, frankly, I am tired of being scared. Honestly, right now, I don't even know how I'm supposed to make a living, but I've thought about all you told me last week . . . especially all that about setting standards according to the results I want to achieve. Okay then, I'll figure out the *how* later, but right now I am quite certain about the results I want for my family. Okay. I'm ready to learn and move. So, if you will, mark me down for an *extraordinary* life."

"Done," Jones said. "Consider yourself on the list." Turning to look at the older house behind us, Jones gestured toward it and said, "I need to be in there in a bit. It's almost noon."

I looked at the house and wondered about Jones's appointment. What could that be? I also wondered how he had connected with Baker. After a mental detour away from the conversation, I zoned back in.

"I know we haven't much time," Jones was saying to Baker, "but there are several quick things I want to convey. You are determining to think differently in order to achieve different results, correct?" Baker agreed. "Okay . . . about the credit thing. Would a life without debt of any kind be extraordinary?"

"Ah . . . yes," Baker said, trying not to show his doubt about that possibility so soon after he had told Jones that he wanted an extraordinary life.

"Good, I agree," Jones said. "Question: Last week, had your credit been good, would you have gotten a loan? For something?"

"Probably," Baker admitted.

"Yes," Jones agreed again. "Most people would have in your situation. Of course, if you had, you would have been right back in debt. In essence, you would have moved away from—in the opposite direction from—the life you just chose to pursue.

"Look at it from this perspective: a situation that looks like a bad thing to most folks—you can't get a loan—is now a good thing if you can manage to think differently."

Baker nodded as the old man continued. "Son, you just stated that a life without debt would be extraordinary. An extraordinary life is a destination. In order for you to arrive at that chosen destination at some point in the future, it is critical that you choose the correct pathway to *begin* that journey. There are many pathways from which to choose, but only one pathway will lead to the destination you desire.

"It is a paradox for the ages. How we think determines how wisely we choose; yet, at the same time, we are able to choose how we think."

Jones stood and motioned for Baker to join him. I stood, too, and followed the direction of the old man's bony finger. He was indicating a huge ship several miles away out in the bay. It was easily spotted from our hill. The high vantage point yielded a perfect view.

"It's a container vessel leaving the Port of Mobile," Jones said. "Where do you think it's going?"

"I don't know," Baker answered. "I guess it could be anywhere."

"Yes, it could be anywhere," Jones agreed. "I'll tell you what, though . . . I'll bet the captain knows exactly where."

Baker nodded and smiled at what seemed like an offhand remark, a joke. But it was no joke, as Jones was about to make clear.

"You see," Jones said to Baker, "before that ship ever left port, the captain knew without any doubt exactly where he was headed. But to have any hope of reaching that destination, he was required to make a specific decision before he pulled away from the dock. It was the answer to a very simple question: In which direction do we head?

"There are shipping lanes to the east, west, north, south, and every variation of those four directions that crisscross the globe. But let's say the captain of that ship intends to reach Sydney, Australia, without delay. Well, from Mobile, Alabama, there is only one choice. And with all the variables of weather, foreign conflict, fuel, and delivery agreements, he needed to make a wise choice, and that choice had to have been made before the journey began.

"Baker, you are at the beginning of your journey to a worthy destination that *you* have chosen. You must now place yourself on the correct path to that place. How will you choose to think at the beginning of your journey?

"Will you choose to think, 'Oh, my situation is horrible; I can't even get a loan'? Or will your perspective be, 'Knowing that I would rather live an extraordinary life sooner rather than later, I will choose to be grateful for my current situation. Fortunately my current situation is one in which I can learn discipline and be trained to live in such a way that will prepare me for the very future I have chosen'?

"If you can see this situation in its correct form, you will understand that you have been given the advantage of a head start. You are favorably positioned in a game that must be won before receiving the reward of an extraordinary life.

"Most people will play that game while doing constant battle against the temptation of debt and the easy road it seems to offer at the beginning of the journey. But you, my friend, will not have to fight that fight." Jones grinned and punched Baker lightly on the shoulder. "Consider yourself blessed, young man. You couldn't get a loan if you had to!"

They laughed a bit as Baker became comfortable with the idea of a new thought process. He was excited despite the fact that he felt strange doing a one-eighty on some things he had assumed were true his entire life. Or maybe the change in direction was the very reason for his excitement. *After all*, Baker thought, *the road I chose years ago surely didn't end well.*

"When you learn to live a disciplined life financially," Jones added, "you are able to live your life as one who leads others to the knowledge of how to sail above the rough seas created by economic conditions or a family member's health . . ."

"Or the weather," Baker said.

"Or the weather," Jones repeated before moving closer to the trunk of the huge oak tree. "Come over here, you two," he said to us, and of course, we did as he asked. Experience had taught him that changing location in the middle of a time of learning would often cement the lesson in the mind of a student. Even a small move was often enough. "My old bones can't stay in one place too long. Big tree, ain't it?" He patted the huge trunk, we agreed, and he continued.

"Fellas," he said, "here's a word to remember: *value*. It's a concept not often understood. Most people equate value with money, and money does have value. But the highest value—the most important value—is the value you create with your life and how you use it for others.

"Here is a good example. Baker, I know you are curious about Jack Bailey. When I met Jack . . ." Jones paused and looked at me. "I met Jack a short time after I met Andy. Jack was a lot like you are right now, Baker, in that he was just beginning to create the life he enjoys today.

"You see them as wealthy, and I certainly understand why,

but the Baileys, and people like them whom I *most* admire, do not obtain their senses of self from the things they have. Their worth is in who they have become. But get this . . . who they *have become*—their personal and business reputations—have been greatly shaped by how they create value for others. And these folks are able to do even more for others with the things they have.

"Baker, the man you become will be determined by the value you provide for others—those whom you meet on the road to who you are becoming. Great or small, your legacy will be judged one day by the quality and amount of value you were able to contribute in the lives of other people.

"Therefore, you should work hardest on yourself in order that you become more valuable. Not *for* yourself, of course, or as an exercise in ego, but that one day you might find yourself valuable enough to possess the power to lead others to an understanding of the true value of their own lives."

With that, Jones looked at the sun and said, "Gotta go." He quickly shook our hands, walked up the steps of the old house, opened the door, and walked inside. Baker and I looked at each other with our eyebrows raised and chuckled as we shook our heads.

We stood and talked for a while about our backgrounds and families. I encouraged him about his current situation and told him a couple of my Jones stories. About fifteen minutes had passed, and Baker was about to say something when he glanced at his watch. "Oh, no!" he exclaimed. "I'm late to pick up my wife." He shook my hand quickly and said, "Nice to meet you." As he trotted away, he called out over his shoulder, "Hope to see you soon."

I stood there under the tree and watched him as he walked toward town, finally rounding a corner several blocks away. Only then did I turn to gaze thoughtfully at the house Jones had entered a while ago. An appointment? What kind of an appointment does one have in a house, especially one that old and in such disrepair? I wasn't sure and would not even hazard a guess. It bothered me that I couldn't or didn't want to guess, and I wondered if my imagination was gone altogether. That would explain not coming up with a story for my book.

In addition, I recognized that, evidently, I had developed a degree of strange pride in the fact that Jones had helped me all those many years ago. He had found me. He had chosen *me*. And I had done okay. Now, all of a sudden, I find out he helped Jack Bailey too? Wow! Jack Bailey was big time. Wealth, influence . . . as far as I could see, the man had done way more than "okay." I had met him on a couple of occasions, and there was no doubt that Jack Bailey was as great a guy as you would ever want to meet. So why did I feel so deflated?

I walked back to the car and officially announced my depression to myself. In addition—and this was somehow scary—for the first time ever, Jones had given me horrible advice. Terrible, useless, ridiculous advice. Write a book and structure the whole thing around a story of normal, boring, everyday life? Yeah, right.

With that in my mind, I turned around and walked back to the old house. I wasn't sure why . . . Perhaps I needed another conversation with Jones. Maybe I was hoping he would give me a specific answer regarding my book. For whatever reason, though, I was oddly compelled to see Jones.

Right then.

Fourteen

I climbed the steps and, not seeing a doorbell, simply knocked. An old man—not the one I was looking for—came to the door, opened it about a foot, and stared. Before I could say a word, he scowled deeply and began to close the door.

Suddenly I heard my friend's familiar voice. "Andy?" His call came from the back of the house, barely reaching me from around the man who was shutting the door in my face.

"Hey, Jones!" I said, half-yelling into the narrowing opening. The man stopped pushing the door but looked at me with what I assumed was his nastiest expression. I stood there, and so did he. Nothing happened for several seconds, but then my old friend came into view and moved up behind the man.

"It's okay," Jones told him, and slowly, the man opened the door and stepped aside. With a motion from my friend, I stepped inside the old house, keeping an eye on the guy who looked as if he would love to tear me apart.

Jones turned with a motion of his head, indicating I should follow. I started to do just that, but the man still at the door, still looking as angry as anyone I've ever seen, said, "Wait." So I stopped and waited, though for what I had no clue.

Fifteen seconds passed, then twenty. At what I figure was the thirty-second mark, Jones came back into the room. He stopped, looked at me, and seemed to assess the situation before turning to the man and saying, "Yes, Darrel. It's him. Now come on."

Jones left again. I didn't move because the man had not moved. My mind was racing. I had no idea what I had gotten myself into.

When he spoke, he asked, "You are?"

My instinct for self-preservation was urging me to yell, "No, I am not!" and run as fast as I could from this house that was becoming crazier by the moment. Instead, I calmly put the onus back upon my scary host. "Are what?" I asked.

"You are the author?" he clarified. "The one who writes the stories?"

"Yes sir," I responded, figuring that must have been what Jones had just confirmed for him. "Yes sir," I said again. "I guess that's me."

Once more I waited as he stared at me. Finally he slowly nodded, and the scowl eased a bit. "She loved your books," he said, and a tear tracked down his old cheek. He made no effort to wipe it from his face. He stepped toward the doorway into which I had seen Jones disappear and as he passed me, quietly said, "Please . . ."

I followed him down a short hallway, past photographs as old as the house, and into a tiny room. Jones was in a chair in the corner. I could see him around the man's shoulder though the rest of the room was still blocked from my view. Jones was smiling as if we were watching children sail homemade boats in a park. The man, however—Darrel or whoever he was—moaned softly when he entered the room and, after only a few steps, fell to his knees.

I stopped immediately and stayed where I was. Darrel was less than five feet away, on his knees with his back to me. Jones remained in the corner chair and was facing my direction.

Between the two men was a bed holding an old woman who lay quietly with her eyes closed.

For some reason, with my first glimpse of the scene before me, I thought of the story all of us hear as children. I saw the hero. Stalwart and enduring, the prince was right in front of me, kneeling beside the bed of the woman who was to him the most precious ever created. And now, still so in love after all these years, the prince—with every fiber in his being—was willing his sleeping beauty to wake up . . . wake up immediately and leave this place so that they might live together, happily ever after.

But this was not a fairy tale. Darrel was old, yes, but he was also physically worn out. I had seen that in his eyes and on his skin and in the way he moved. And the woman, quite simply, was dying. I could see that she was alive at the moment, but the room smelled of death. What was Jones doing here? What was I doing here?

Darrel looked up, across the bed, and fixed Jones with a stare. I could not see his face, but I could feel his anger. "You keep coming back," he said.

Jones smiled gently and nodded. "Yes, I do."

"Even though I have cursed you," Darrel said. "Even though I have not asked for your help, you keep coming back," I heard him say. Then, a question: "What do you want from me?"

Jones tilted his head and said, "I have never wanted anything from you, Darrel. But there has been so much I have wanted *for* you."

I saw Darrel's head turn slightly. He was looking at the woman. "She always liked you."

"She has been a wonderful wife for you," Jones said, and the man sobbed.

"Everything's over now," Darrel said.

I was listening intently, watching everything. When the man on his knees in front of me said that everything was over,

I saw Jones's eyes narrow slightly. "Why would you believe that, Darrel?" he asked.

"Because she is dying!" he bellowed. "She will soon be gone. Gone! Dead!"

I was startled when the man yelled, and now he was really scaring me. This was getting out of control. I was about to back out of the room when Jones stood, reached across the woman, and touched Darrel on the arm. Darrel looked at my old friend and was instantly calm, quiet. It was weird.

Jones looked at the woman but spoke to the man. "Would you like to know the truth, Darrel?" he said. "Would you like to know what she is experiencing . . . what is really happening right now?"

"I don't know if I do or not," he answered in a trembling voice.

Well, I thought, *that is as honest a reply as you'll ever hear.*

"I believe you do want to know," Jones said. "You need to know." Then Jones looked at me. "And I wanted you to hear this too. I want you to write about it . . ."

I nodded but was uneasy. What was this? In the past Jones had barely acknowledged that I write. He had never suggested a topic. The one time I had asked for advice, I didn't get it. Now he actually has something he *wants* me to write? What might this be? What truth?

Suddenly I wasn't sure if I wanted to hear this or not either. I looked at the woman on the bed, and I saw my mother. I don't mean that she looked like her. The woman in front of me was much older than my mom, who had been only forty-two when she died. But the smell of the room and the helpless anger inside it were exactly the same. Many nights I had lain awake on the floor in my mother's bedroom. Hour after hour I would listen to her cough, but it was not her coughing that frightened me. No, I dreaded the silence I knew was coming. I dreaded the moment when the coughing would stop.

"Darrel," Jones began, "you think that your sweet wife is at the end, but that is only a lie you have believed. Because *your* fear has grown, you believe *her* fear has become greater . . . which is another lie. You believe she is experiencing something bad that gets worse until there is nothing at all. That, too, is a lie.

"Here is the truth, Darrel. She is not at the end. She is at the beginning. Her fear has not become greater; it has become less and less until now, her fear is gone altogether. And she is not experiencing something bad that gets worse until there is nothing at all . . . she is experiencing something incredible that gets better, until there is everything."

Jones looked down at the woman and lightly touched her head. "Before this woman was ever born, when she was warm and snug inside her mama's belly, she kicked and twisted, moving this way and that. For months she struggled. She became uncomfortable. She longed for more freedom and began to sense that the world she inhabited was not where she ultimately belonged. She did not know what was on the other side of her struggle, but she was getting ready to experience something new and wonderful that in her wildest imaginings could not be described. Darrel . . . she was getting ready to breathe.

"And when she finally drew that first breath, it was clean and fresh and like nothing she had ever felt. She took another breath and another—and all around her, loved ones and friends cheered in a joyous celebration of her arrival."

Jones looked closely at the woman's face. "Look at her now, Darrel," he said. "For many years this dear child was happy and content in *this* body. But for some time now, she has struggled. She has become uncomfortable. She has begun to long for freedom from the pain of this body and has sensed that the world she inhabits is not where she ultimately belongs. Even now she does not fully appreciate the reality that is waiting on the other side of her struggle, but she is preparing to experience something new and wonderful that in her wildest imaginings could not be described. Right now . . . right this minute . . . she is getting ready to breathe.

"And when she draws that first breath, it will be clean and clear and fresh, like nothing she has ever experienced. She will take another breath and another and another; and all around, her loved ones, her family and friends, will cheer in a joyous celebration of her arrival.

"Do not be afraid for yourself, Darrel. You can make the same journey one day—you can join her if you choose to do so. And don't be afraid for her. She is fine. Remember . . . she is getting ready to breathe."

After a time of quiet Jones slipped out of the room, and I followed, leaving Darrel alone with the woman. He was still on his knees with his upper body on the bed. He held her hand and was peacefully asleep.

It was a serenity he had not felt in a long time. Somehow Darrel's mind drifted easily through the years as he dreamed of the past he remembered and a future he had never allowed himself to imagine.

Fifteen

Sealy loved Baker, and she was well aware that her thinking and her choices had also contributed to the mess they were in. *No,* Sealy reminded herself, *this is not a mess we are in. This is a mess we are working our way out of.* Then, to herself, Sealy repeated the words Jones had suggested she make her own: *I am choosing to think differently. I am choosing to see my situation with perspective. When I find perspective, I establish power over my current circumstances.*

She and Baker had talked themselves to sleep almost every night lately, and one of the constant themes was their thinking. More than a couple of times, Sealy had heard Jones discuss the way people think. Then Baker had spent a whole day with Jack Bailey, an incredible man Jones arranged for Baker to meet. Baker had told her that Jack Bailey also talked about how folks think.

All those ideas were new to Baker and Sealy, but for Sealy, it took longer to process. She was getting there, however, and it was making a difference already. It was just that the stories Baker had told her lately all seemed so fantastic . . . especially the one about Jones in the field the first day. Maybe *unreal* would be a better word for the stories, she had thought. But Baker was already a new person, full of hope and ideas, and for that, she was grateful.

Perhaps the incredible yarns and their recent frequency had taken their toll, but for whatever reason, Sealy laughed in Baker's face when he told her there was a five-pound goldfish in the Grand Hotel's pond. "Oh, Baker, give me a break," she'd said and rolled her eyes.

Minutes later, as she almost lost her shoe to a patch of sticky mud, Sealy would have given anything to take back those words. Maybe it was the eye roll that had placed her in this position. *Ugh*, Sealy thought. *Why didn't I say something like, "Five pounds? Wow!"?*

It wasn't that she didn't enjoy seeing the goldfish; Sealy's aggravation with herself was that she had known better. All women knew better. The situation in which Sealy found herself thirty seconds after getting out of their car could have been avoided because it was all wrapped up in the natural defensiveness that Baker possessed as a man. The fact that he was a typical man meant that he was of course *hugely* offended if ever a shadow of uncertainty was cast upon anything he said. And one could triple the reaction if it happened to be the man's poor wife who had innocently voiced the doubt.

That offhand remark had prompted Baker to insist that without delay, she walk around the pond with him until he spotted the monstrous escapee from some kid's aquarium. It was on the third trip around that he had (Thank God!) finally seen it, and she'd said, "Yes! Wow! You were right! That's unbelievable!" all the while knowing full well that she would have reported having seen the creature from the black lagoon if it meant she wouldn't have to circle the pond again.

It was almost six thirty when they climbed the bank from the pond to the parking lot. They were headed to the pier, and Baker had already said, "See? I told you," at least five times when a young woman got out of the coolest minibus Sealy had ever seen.

"Whoa!" Baker exclaimed before Sealy could say anything. "What is that?"

"Hi, guys!" the young woman greeted them brightly. "Do you love it?"

"That is so great!" Sealy said. "What is that color? It has a sky-blue . . . aquamarine, smoky thing going on."

"Palladian Blue is the official name of the color," Christy said. "Benjamin Moore HC-144. And it's a camper too! This is going to be my photography vehicle." She held out her hand. "I'm Christy Haynes . . . BeachChicPhotography.com. We live in Orange Beach, but I travel. Tell me your names . . ."

"What?" Baker asked, and Sealy laughed.

Baker was overwhelmed, and Sealy knew it. "I'm Sealy Larson," she said. "This is my husband, Baker. He likes your van, and he'll catch up in a minute and probably talk about it. We have two teenage daughters, and Baker tends to shut down when we all talk at once." She laughed again. "We're here to meet a man who is helping us. Evidently there is a class—"

"Jones?" Christy said. "That's why I'm here too!"

Soon they were hurrying from the parking lot to the pier, where Jones was waiting. Sealy and Christy were giggling like schoolgirls when they reached the end. Baker shrugged an "I have no idea" to Jones as they approached. Jones smiled, and Baker realized suddenly how good he felt right at that moment. His wife was happy. For the first time, maybe ever, he had a direction, and a new life was waiting for him to shape and mold with good choices.

"Girls? Children?" Jones teased as he motioned for Christy and Sealy to join where he and Baker were already sitting. As they took their seats, Jones remarked, "I'm not even going to ask what that was about." Of course that set them off again. When at last the two women had gained some semblance of control, Jones said, "I asked you to come a bit early tonight. Several others will arrive after a while, but I have a guest who'll be here in a few moments just for you. Quickly, before he arrives, I'd like to know what you are looking to do for a living."

"Photography," Christy blurted out. "I already have my website. It's BeachChicPhotography.com. Isn't that a cool name? I don't have the camera I really need yet, though. I mean, the one I have is fine. It's just not the very—"

"Thank you, Christy," Jones interrupted. Baker looked as if he might jump over the pier railing. "Sealy? What are you looking to do?"

Suddenly shy, Sealy wondered if her idea was ridiculous and hesitated. "Go, Sealy!" Christy said and made her new friend smile.

"Okay . . . ," Sealy began. "Well . . . I love plants, and I see nice houses all the time whose flowerbeds are empty or uncared for. I'm pretty good at growing things . . .

"Baker?" she said to her husband. "You know how you told me Jones said not to think in an average way?" Baker nodded. "Well, remember last Saturday, when you were at that Mr. Bailey guy's house all day?" Baker nodded again. His mouth was too dry to speak. "I went to sixteen houses while you were gone. I was able to talk to eleven of the owners. I told them how nice their yards would look if some of the beds I saw were planted and cared for.

"Every single one of them told me they already had a person or a landscape service taking care of their yards, but I remembered what you said Jones told you about value. So I told them that my business did not do landscape, that I specialized in seasonal beds. I said that for a certain amount, I would plant, fertilize, trim, prune, mulch, and change the beds completely three times a year. I said that all *they* would be required to do . . . I told them, 'All I will need you to do is drive in and out of your driveway, looking at your incredible yard and accepting all the compliments from your neighbors."

Christy was about to jump out of her chair but managed to stay quiet. Jones was grinning, but Baker asked the question they all wanted Sealy to answer. "Did anybody say yes?"

"Eight of them did, Baker," Sealy said. "Eight of them. I have almost three thousand dollars already on the books. I don't have books yet, of course, but that's what you say when you're in business, right, 'on the books'? I already gave my notice at the restaurant, Baker. The girls are resigning too. I've got to have help."

He avoided fainting, but Baker was lightheaded as he went through the motions of informing the others about his business interest. "Cooking," he said. "Cooking . . . like outdoor-style. I mean good things, though, not just steaks and burgers. So . . . cooking."

Jones was about to speak when Baker added, "Fishing too. Also working on boats and motors. And by that, I mean *boat* motors. So boats and boat motors, fishing, and cooking."

Jones did not delay. "What else?" he asked. "And think in terms of the value your passion has for other people." He looked at the dark-haired young woman first. "Christy?"

"Okay," she started, "I'll try to do this quickly. Value. I think I get this. Not who would hire me as a photographer or who will let me take their pictures and pay me because anyone could do that, right?" She was talking to Jones, who nodded slowly. She was on the right track.

"So . . . there is a specific camera—and when I get the money, this is the one I'll have—this camera, if used correctly, can produce photographs that are startling in their intensity. I am telling you . . . photographs of a family or a child in the right photographer's hands . . . of course, it is really the photographer's eye that makes it all work . . ."

Jones glanced at Sealy and Baker. Both were smiling, and Sealy, especially, was interested in what Christy was saying.

"Anyway, here's the value: I will work with specific interior designers . . ." Christy stopped her monologue in its tracks, looked at Sealy, and said, "Oh my gosh! Do you know Melanie Martin in Orange Beach? She owns M Two. Unbelievable interiors. Your plant thing? She is going to *love* your idea!"

After patting Sealy on the leg, Christy continued to talk. "Jones," she said, "with interior designers such as Melanie as clients or even individuals who contact my website—it's BeachChicPhotography .com, did I already tell you that?—anyway, I will create framed wall galleries from photographs wrapped on canvas. These will be made to fit whatever specific wall space a person or company desires. The pieces and multiple-frame galleries I will produce are not available anywhere else!

"Think about it . . . This business will provide select clients with a limited-edition gallery—a number one, of one. Ha! How's that for limited? Anyway, what was I saying? Oh! This will be a limited-edition gallery . . . no! It will be a *one-of-a-kind* wall gallery of a person's life or family or their children. The gallery will be created by a special photographic process and produced by hand for a specific location in someone's home. What do you think?"

"I think you are on to something," Jones said. "Terrific start. I love it. Sealy, I love your idea about the plants too!"

Baker was overwhelmed and a little nervous that she and the girls were quitting their jobs, but he was excited and proud of his wife. The value Sealy found for someone else in what she loved to do was remarkable. She had proven the value to other people, and now she actually had clients. It was nothing more, Baker decided, than perspective—a different way of thinking about something about which everyone had already been aware for years. With that kind of thinking, Sealy had opened a business of her own—and created jobs—in a single day.

The shy woman to whom he had been married for years now had Baker looking at his own ideas through a new lens. "The ideas I have can be proven too," he said to Jones, "just like Sealy already did. Just hearing her story has already changed what I know I can do. What she did by actually selling her idea—proving its value— is the same thing I can do.

"One thing, I want to allow a few specific people who own great boats to have their own personal boat mechanic. Do you know how long it takes around here to get a boat repair done? It's ridiculous. And I just *know* there are at least a few folks who would be thrilled to pay a modest monthly fee in order to have a mechanic virtually on-call for them.

"I'll work out a fishing service too. There are lots of people around here who have boats but don't know how or where to fish. I know how and where, but I don't have a boat. I can prove value to those people, I promise. Then after a day fishing on their boat, with my third business I will creatively cook their dinner, using the fish they caught as the main course. Guess how I'll cook it?" Baker said to Sealy.

"On your Kamado Joe," she said.

"Of course!" Baker responded. "I've already drawn the plans for an open trailer that holds an outdoor kitchen . . . with three BigJoe grills on it. I'll eventually have to get two more, of course, but this will work. It's totally different from what the usual caterer does."

From behind him, Baker heard a man's voice. "I already know how to fish, and I can cook them, too, but if you'll tell me how much you need for the personal mechanic service, I'll sign the deal right now."

It was Jack Bailey.

"There it is!" Polly screamed, and I almost ran our car into the Grand Hotel's pond.

The object of Polly's attention was a forty-year-old, aqua-colored Volkswagen minibus parked between a Corvette and a Mercedes. "That's Christy's van!" Polly squealed as I, with great skill and nerves of steel, managed to park nearby.

It was Thursday evening, and we were early again for Jones's third parenting class. Only twenty minutes ahead of schedule, we did not have enough time to eat—in fact, we had grabbed a bite on the way—but we did have just enough time to look at the van. "Come on," Polly urged as I stuck my face in front of the last moment of air conditioning I would enjoy until later in the evening.

Groaning at the prospect of being forced to look at an old van, I exited our own vehicle and walked toward what my wife was already describing out loud as "a work of art, a thing of beauty, an antique of great historical significance . . ."

Not being a car person myself, upon stepping into the presence of greatness not seen as a means of transport since the shuttle program at NASA, I could only muster, "Very nice."

"Dear!" She seemed stunned by my nonchalance. "Dear, this is a Westie! It's an original VW Microbus with the Westfalia Camper addition. Come here and look inside. This is fabulous."

Hm, I thought. *Fabulous? From a woman who would not camp if the lives of her children depended upon it?* At her insistence I looked through the louvered side windows.

"It has a sink," she said, "and a stove and a fridge and a little closet."

It did indeed. And with the pop-top featuring a hanging bunk, I could not resist a smidgen of sarcasm. "Wow! This *is* great," I said.

"See?" Polly responded, biting hard on the little piece of bait I had dangled in front of her. "I told you it was incredible."

"Oh yeah," I smirked, "and with all these cool additions I'll bet you could cram an entire half of a person in there. Can a half person drive this thing?"

Polly did not speak to me as we walked to the hotel's pier. I was snickering just loudly enough for her to hear, so I'm sure that had something to do with it, but by the time we arrived three minutes later, all was good. "Christy is already out there," she observed. "And Jones. And . . ."

"That's Baker Larson," I said, "the guy I met with Jones the other day. And that'd be his wife with him, I suppose."

Polly stared. "And there's someone else."

"That someone else is Jack Bailey," I said, a bit surprised. "I wonder what he's doing here."

Polly had an idea. "You know, I've talked to Christy several times lately. She said that she was meeting before class with Jones. Something about business, remember? They mentioned it last week."

"I remember," I said. "Baker needs something. And, hey, if they're meeting about business, Jones has the right guy out there in Jack Bailey. He lives within a mile of here," I added, looking around.

"It's that way," Polly pointed. "I went to a ladies' charity event there once. I'm not sure I could find the driveway again, but it's an unbelievable place. And I *loved* her . . . his wife, Mary Chandler." I nodded.

We had stopped in the late afternoon shade of one of the massive oaks beside the Grand Hotel's Conference Center. Quiet for a while, we were content to watch the small group from a distance. "Jack's doing most of the talking," Polly finally said.

"I noticed that too," I said. "Look at Jones. Leaning on the rail with his arms crossed . . . See how he's smiling? What's happening?"

"Hey!" Baker said when he saw his friend and jumped up to shake his hand. Baker introduced Jack to Sealy and Christy before turning to Jones and asking, "Jack is our guest?"

"Yes, he is," Jones replied. "And we have only a little time before the others arrive." He beckoned them toward the pier railing and said, "Let's move over here and catch the breeze. Jack, if you don't mind, talk for five or six minutes on how to outdo your competition in business. You are somewhat on down the road with your businesses. Your perspective on how it all happened will be interesting."

Jack was about to begin by saying that Jones had been the first man in his life who had loved him enough to tell him the truth about himself. He intended to inform the small class about having walked around town all day one Sunday, then all day Monday, before he finally ran into the old man on that Tuesday morning. He wanted to say that he would have spent any amount or paid any price for the fifteen minutes he had gotten to spend with Jones.

These people in front of him included a man who was now a friend of his own. They were starting businesses, and Jack wanted to express just how important the wisdom and thinking aspect of their lives would be if they expected to succeed. It had been Jones, he planned to say, who was responsible for whatever success he had attained.

Actually, Jack had a lot to say before he started on the topic that had been requested, but when he opened his mouth to speak, the old man spoke first. "Jack?" he said.

"Yes sir?"

"In the limited time we have," Jones said, "dig as deep as you can into adding value to the lives of others and the extreme business advantage that particular focus provides. And Jack?"

"Sir?" Jack answered as Jones smiled at him.

"Leave me out of it."

At that moment the thought raced through Jack's consciousness that he—Jack Bailey—had traveled the world and was a well-respected member of his community, a leader . . . How was it then, he wondered, that he could be so easy to read and out-maneuvered by this particular old man?

Jack shifted his mental gears quickly and said, "I have learned that it is relatively easy to beat the competition. We do this by playing at a level at which most people are not even aware there is a game going on. A consistent winner in any endeavor thinks differently—sometimes dramatically so—than ordinary people. Our competition tends to focus on their business. What can we do to attract attention? How can we get more customers? Unfortunately for them, the more they focus upon themselves, the further they push away from their ultimate objective, which is to grow and prosper."

Christy was frowning. "Wait," she said. "If you don't focus on your own business, what do you focus on?"

"Other people," Jack said, but the answer did not erase Christy's frown, so he explained. "I have learned that one can create value in people's lives that goes beyond what they think of as 'your business.'

"It is possible to create value in the lives of other people, some of whom might not even be clients or customers; that is more important to them than what your business actually provides.

When that is accomplished, that person will never hire, work with, or buy from anyone else."

Now it was Baker's turn to frown. "I'm not sure I get it. Can you give an example of how you create that kind of value?"

"Yes," Jack replied, "and I could give you one example after another for hours. But here is one. It was something we did at our car dealerships.

"You need to understand that most folks shop for cars by price, and they generally don't like the process. Prices fluctuate, of course, and sometimes people will spend two hundred dollars in gas, driving around to different dealerships in order to save three hundred dollars on the purchase of a car."

Baker smiled. "Yeah, I might have done that a time or two myself."

Jack continued. "So the vast majority of people feel a bit of an adversarial relationship with car dealers. Now, if a dealer has been in a place for a long time, as we have, there is a greater opportunity to have developed long-lasting relationships with customers. Some of our customers don't shop anywhere else."

Sealy understood. "They are your friends. You've proven yourself over time, and they have become your friends."

"Correct," Jack said. "But what about the people we *don't* know? To create that kind of loyalty in them seems impossible on the surface. This is where we learned to compete at a different level.

"Several years ago there was an industry-wide slump. Folks were simply not buying cars. And it wasn't just us; all dealerships were suffering during a national economic downturn. Even heading into the holiday season, which is traditionally a good time for us, it was bleak. Knowing that December did not appear promising and deciding we would not sit around and mope, we began working for our longtime customers *and* those potential customers who would be making decisions in the future.

"We put ads on radio, in print, and online, but not a single one was about prices or a sale. We told a truth that consumers rarely hear, and it got their attention. We said, 'Business is slow, and we have time on our hands during the Christmas season!' The next line was, 'We want to give that time to you, the members of our community.' The rest of the ad or radio spot or whatever told them exactly what we were going to do.

"We moved the majority of our service people into the showroom with their tools, and there, until Christmas Eve, the mechanics, the salespeople, the receptionist, and yours truly spent all day, every day, and on into most of the nights, putting together toys for anyone who wanted our help."

"Ha!" Christy exclaimed. "Really?"

"Yep, really. We did not charge a dime. No tipping was allowed. We had doughnuts and coffee for people who wanted to wait, or they could go shopping and come back anytime. I have no idea how many bicycles I put together that December, but let me tell you something, I could put one together in my sleep now."

They all laughed.

"Anyway, here's what happened. People were grateful. We were excited because of the folks we had helped. It was an incredible Christmas for us. We didn't sell many cars, but that didn't matter. We always make our decisions based on long-term benefits. Operation Christmas Toys was exactly that. And it was fun. We've done it twice more since."

"You didn't sell many cars?" Baker asked, confused. "I thought you were giving us an example of something that worked . . . something that helped you rise above the competition."

"Oh, I just meant we didn't sell many cars *then*," Jack said slyly. "When that industry slump ended and folks began buying cars again, it seemed like they were buying them all from us.

"All that shopping for the best price? Seeing what dealership would go a hundred dollars lower than the other guy? None of that mattered anymore to the folks we had helped. You see, Baker, by adding value to people's lives beyond their traditional thoughts about our business, we made quite a few friends. Those friends decided where they would buy their next car well in advance of actually needing one."

"Unbelievable," Baker said.

"Not really," Jack countered. "People want to be treated well. They've come not to expect it, but they'd still like for it to happen. I decided years ago that no one would ever be treated or welcomed or honored anywhere or by anyone better than they would be treated when they ran into me, whether I was 'on the job' or not. This wasn't even necessarily a business thing. It was a life decision for me that turned into a business asset."

"Can you throw another story in here, Jack?" Jones asked. "We have a little more than two minutes."

"Sure," Jack responded. "We also own a few restaurants. All of them serve to capacity, lunch and dinner, six days a week. The food is fresh and well prepared, but a lot of dining establishments manage that. Curiously, we only began packing the places when we added one behavior to the culture of our team.

"Our waitstaff, cooks, and management learned the names of a number of their occasional customers. Those occasional customers became regular customers. They are a better advertisement than we could ever afford. That might seem a small thing to you and me, but it's a big thing to people who are not often welcomed enthusiastically at work, at church, or even in their own homes. Huge value.

"Quickly, here's another. I hope this doesn't sound like bragging, but I want you to understand how profitable doing the right thing can be. Our real estate companies sell more real estate than their competitors by far. That is the case in every market we are in. Why? Well, selling real estate is what everyone does, so we do that too. And we do it well. In addition, again, we are striving to compete on a level that the competition is not even aware a game is being played.

"So every day we diligently seek to discover ways of adding value to the lives of our customers and our *potential* customers. We seek value that goes beyond traditional real estate. Once we accomplish that, not only have we added value to the lives of deserving people, we have created a business advantage that is hard to put one's finger on and impossible for the competition to advertise against."

Baker asked, "What do you mean, 'impossible to advertise against'?"

"What could the competition possibly say?" Jack grinned. "Can't you see the billboard? 'We are aware that the friend you love and adore is in the real estate business, but please, let us sell your home instead!'"

Christy, Sealy, and Baker clapped as Jack said a brief thanks and hugged Jones. He shook their hands and reminded Baker to come by his house with the details about the personal mechanic service. Jack also encouraged Sealy and Christy before waving again and walking past a group from Jones's parenting class that was now arriving.

Sixteen

When we saw the small meeting coming to an end, Polly and I began walking toward the pier. I had intended to speak to Jack Bailey, but he reached the sidewalk without seeing us and turned the other way. Seeing also that Jones was gathering everyone at the end of the pier, I decided I could say hello to Jack another time, and we hurried on out.

We were the last two to arrive. Glancing about, I saw that our semicircle was arranged, and we were arranged in it, as we had been the week before, with one minor exception. Baker and Sealy had joined us. Polly and Christy had talked by phone several times during the past week. I had observed Christy and Sealy together already. Now, all three were sitting together: Polly, Christy, and Sealy. *Good luck, Jones*, I thought. *I hope you get to talk tonight . . .*

Kelli and Bart were on the far end of the group, Kelli sitting next to Baker. Kelli started our evening by reviewing our twenty-one desired parenting results. When she finished reading the list, we all looked to Jones. The sky was dark and threatening. It had been overcast all day. There was no immediate forecast of rain, but low clouds over the bay always seem to compress the salty humidity, and I could taste the air.

"Allow me to review what we know and present a few conclusions," Jones said. "The conclusions, I believe, should produce the results you desire for the future of your children. As always, questions are welcome."

Jones stopped for just a moment before continuing to speak. I wasn't sure why. Perhaps he was waiting on a question. I felt certain he had not lost his place. It was not even a long pause, merely something I noticed.

"From our previous discussions," Jones said, "we determined that today's society has come to an amiable impasse regarding the different standards by which its children are raised. During our time together, we have come to understand that while most parents are doing the best they can, there is no consensus—no societal agreement—about a standard.

"And there is complacency, an acceptance of what is, that affects human beings. That complacency encourages a person to disengage from the effort to shape the culture in which he lives.

"Sometimes we wonder why society has become complacent. Society is nothing more than individuals living in close proximity to each other. Society is people. What we refer to as 'culture' is defined by the customs and accepted practices of those people. Therefore, society becomes complacent as a result of individuals giving in to the belief that nothing can be done about their culture. This is not only untrue but also dangerous to believe.

"Listen carefully. While a culture may be defined by the customs and accepted practices of its people, it is critical to understand that it is the *thinking* of its people that creates a culture in the first place. Knowledge of this difference is so significant as to be the key to life or death for civilizations. Indeed, it has been for thousands of years."

Jones paused again, but this time I was paying attention. He appeared to be weighing a particular thought or perhaps a choice of words. I was watching him closely because what I had come to think of as "the unreadable expression" was again on his face. I had not seen it often, but it was as unforgettable as it was unreadable. Sadness, love, joy, and anger, all at the same time. Also nearly as strange was the reaction to his expression I had begun to recognize in myself. Again, all at the same time I felt insignificance, power, hope, fear, and awe.

"At this time," Jones finally said, "I feel the moment has come to inform you that the work you will complete during the next few years is critical not only to the future of your own children but also to the future of your nation as well. Unless you want to end up like Rome."

Jones waited as we glanced nervously at each other. Bart, in particular, was frowning deeply.

"The fall of the Roman Empire is a perfect example of what happens to a society that tires of the fight for its children, gives up hope for a cultural standard, and finally agrees to disagree.

"The correct definition of the word *standard* is 'a required or agreed-upon level of quality or attainment.' If that is true, and the definition of the word says that it is, then what today's society has done by agreeing to disagree is to virtually announce that there are *many* standards. Society has proclaimed that a standard is whatever you decide it is.

"But wait . . . A standard is an *agreed-upon* level of quality or attainment. One. One level of quality or attainment that is agreed upon. In other words, when a society grows comfortable with the idea that there can be many standards, the people have, in effect, accepted the reality that there will be *no* standard. Anything goes. And that, my friends, is exactly what happened to a once great, once wealthy, once undefeatable world power.

"Many people tour the ruins of Rome today. Seemingly without exception, they take pictures and wonder aloud how it could have happened. How was it possible, they ask each other, that such an advanced society could have managed to disintegrate, plunging an entire civilization into a darkness and confusion so complete that the world would not escape it for centuries?

"Unfortunately, today, no one seems willing to step up and answer that question. Why is that? Because the answer makes us uncomfortable. If one accepts its truth, the answer *requires* something of us. The answer is nothing if not a dire warning to the very future of our own society."

"What is the answer, Jones?" Bart asked.

"How did Rome manage to collapse?" Jones said. "Historians have written books attempting to answer that question, but the truth? The truth is an uncomplicated story of good people who simply grew tired of promoting and defending what they knew to be right. When the Romans got discouraged and began to move their ideas and values to the outskirts of society, they unwittingly initiated the beginning of the end.

"When one walks the streets of Rome today and imagines the magnificence of that empire at its height, it is important to remember that the glory of Rome was begun with a standard held before her people. The destruction of Rome, however, was begun by *standards* her people held before themselves."

We were all a bit dazed after the beginning of the evening's class. The story of decline and the eventual disappearance of a great nation felt too close to home. Jones looked at us and called a time-out. "Take three minutes," he said, "and we will reconvene."

I wanted to talk to him, but the ladies made a beeline for the old man, getting to him first, and that was that. I saw Polly talking with him as well and went to stand with the other guys. At the end of the break, Bart, Baker, and I were still standing nearby, hoping for a moment with Jones. When that did not happen, as we were about to go to our seats, Bart said to him, "Jones, I think we all are fine to stay as long as you want."

He put a hand on Bart's shoulder and walked him from the railing, where he had been, almost back to Bart's chair. In the seconds it took to cover that small distance, Jones replied, "Thank you, Bart. I appreciate that, but let's see what we can do to cover everything quickly. I believe our time is shorter than one might think." Baker was already seated and talking with Sealy, but I was close by and heard him say it. Bart sort of jerked or twitched as if he had been jabbed with something and looked at me with a "What did he mean by that?" expression on his face. I didn't know.

I do know that I had spent the last three minutes allowing myself to become discouraged again. Yes, even after Jones had explained that kind of thinking could prove problematic. A quick mental review of the different standards our society had already accepted, however, was more than I could take at that moment. As I took my seat, I glanced up at the still-gray sky and thought, *Is there any hope at all?*

"What do we have?" Jones began. "At present, today's society has agreed to disagree. There was, however, one thing we found in our discussions that society does agree on."

I perked up. *Oh?* I thought. *Something society does agree on?*

"Yes," Jones went on, "society agrees that our culture is declining, that we as a people are becoming less than we were. If you examine the top ten problems high school teachers faced with their students of several decades ago versus the top ten problems high school teachers face with the students of today, the differences are chilling. In fact, if today's list were not labeled 'high school,' one might think the list had been created in reference to a prison."

And . . . I am back to no hope.

"But there is hope," Jones said, lending more credence to my suspicion that the old man could read my mind. "There is hope because there is something else society *does* agree upon. And this is a big one."

He had our attention.

"When society looks at its own history and examines the peaks and valleys, there is one particular time we point to as a high-water mark. In the history of our nation, which stretches more than two centuries, one group is always singled out as an example to the rest of us.

"Upon the excellence, character, and integrity of these particular people, everyone agrees. Even among those whose standards might vary greatly from your own, all religious affiliations, members of the media, liberals, conservatives, all races and ages . . . everyone, everywhere, with only a moment to contemplate history and the role of humanity in it, put their fingers squarely in one place and declare, '*That* is the best we ever were.'

"Society acknowledges the cultural rise that preceded that group and the decline in our culture that has occurred since. And still, we point to them. Those people, we say, as we examine that place in our history . . . those people sacrificed more. They served each other more enthusiastically. They cared more about their God and their country. They did not expect to be carried; they offered to carry. They expected to be able to keep most of what they produced. And because of that belief they worked harder and produced more for everyone.

"Yes," Jones said, "society agrees about those people. We even have a name for them. We call them 'the greatest generation.'"

We all had whispered the phrase as Jones spoke it aloud: the greatest generation. He was right; they were. And he was correct in the assertion that everyone agreed that they were. *Still . . . no offense, Jones*, I was thinking, *but so what? How does that help us today?* Truly, I felt we were much closer to Rome than we were to the 1940s and '50s. Then, as he had done so many times before, Jones blew me away.

"I must confess," Jones said, "that I may be the only person you'll ever meet who does *not* believe that those people were 'the best we ever were.' In fact, allow me to state for the record that *I do not believe* that group of people was the greatest generation."

Jones stared at us as we held our breath. What he had just said was so out of bounds we didn't know what to think. He was totally on target with the first part. He had been correct; everyone *does* agree about that one thing. Everyone agrees that those people were the best we ever became. Then he said that they were *not*? I wasn't sure . . . was that sacrilegious?

"No sir," Jones said, "I don't really think those folks deserve the title." He crossed his arms and tilted his head. With his eyes narrowed but still sparkling like blue fire, he said, "If we're really talking *greatest* generation, I'm voting for their mamas and daddies."

Immediately, we understood. A glimmer of hope was beginning to reignite.

Jones got down on one knee as he continued. "I'm thinking that the real heroes of the greatest generation must have been the parents and grandparents who produced them for us. Think! Who raised that generation? Whose standard shaped and molded them as children to become the adults whom society still agrees, decades later, is the greatest representation of humanity ever attained?

"But more importantly for you," Jones said, "more importantly for the future . . . what did they do?"

Jones stood and paced as he thought out loud. "How did

they raise those children? What did those parents expect? What did they require? How did they discipline? And when? What did the kids do after school? Or in the summer?"

"So you think there was a standard at that time?" The question came from Kelli.

"Absolutely, Kelli," Jones replied. "Society, with its multiple standards, has become a game of chance for many parents. The prize is a child who grows into a mature, responsible, productive, happy adult. Think about the possibility that a game of chance like that might produce the greatest generation. You could roll the dice for a thousand years and never come up with results like the parents and grandparents of that time.

"I have no doubt that you and Bart will achieve great results with your children. But the fact remains that your children will not live as adults in a bubble. Your children will live as a part of society whose culture, by any measure, is in a steep decline. They will raise their own families in that society; they will earn their livings there.

"If you people gathered here right now cannot convince others to join you in raising children by a standard that will produce greatness again, your children will be worse off by far than anything you might be experiencing today.

"So was there a standard? Yes, but it was commonly accepted at that time. Your task will be tougher. Remember? There are many standards now, which means it is up to you to make folks listen and persuade them to make a good decision regarding the standard they select."

For about two beats there existed an air of stunned silence. Then, we all talked at once. It was the "up to you" part of what Jones had said that caught our attention.

"Up to us?" Kelli's voice rose above the same chorus being sung by us all. "Up to us?" she asked again as we looked her way.

"Up to us how? My next-door neighbor won't listen to me, and you're talking about 'up to us'?"

Jones didn't answer right away, and Polly jumped in. "I understand what Kelli is saying. I'm afraid this might be a little like converting a person to the other side of the political aisle."

"My husband is a youth minister," Christy said. "It's hard to believe, I know, but we see many different standards by which the teenagers have been raised in our own church. My husband has occasionally asked a kid not to wear a certain thing or talk a certain way. Invariably he will hear from the parent, and the message from the parent is usually, 'It's a matter of opinion. This is our opinion. Stay out of how I raise my kids.'"

Everyone was nodding, agreeing with those who had spoken.

This was very interesting. It appeared to me that Jones had finally lost a round. *Oh well*, I thought. *Jones, you should have stayed with the hypothetical. Once you crossed into that up-to-you territory, the hypothetical became personal. That's where you lost.* But I should have known better. Jones started up again as if he had not heard any of them.

"Most people live under the misconception that it takes a long time to change," Jones said. "This is not true. It can take a long time to *prepare* to change or to *decide* to change or even to *want* to change. Change itself, however, happens in a heartbeat.

"True change—the kind of change that lasts—can be dramatic, but it is totally, one hundred percent predictable."

I looked to my right and left. That last statement had caused eyebrows to rise.

"There are two elements that must be present for a person to change his or her thinking on a matter. It is the thinking, remember, that is our foundation. Okay, two things . . . One, what's in it for me? The first element that must be present for a person to change is an understanding of how that change benefits him or her. What's in it for me? Got it?"

We nodded cautiously.

"The second element that must be in place for a person to execute an immediate and lasting change is . . . proof beyond a logical doubt."

"Logical doubt?" Baker said.

"Beyond a logical doubt," Jones replied. "This does not have to be mathematical proof or some kind of formula; it only needs to be the kind of proof that makes sense to the person."

"But how do we prove a standard?" Bart asked.

"An end result must first be agreed upon," Jones replied. "That's easier than you think. That list of twenty-one results you created? You'd be hard-pressed to find a parent who would not want his or her child to have those qualities as an adult. Once the end result is agreed upon, the process for producing that end result can begin to be determined. This is true whether one is raising a child, advancing a business, or chasing a national championship.

"The process must be refined and tested. Should a particular choice, habit, or activity become part of the process? That answer will be determined by whether or not that choice, habit, or activity moves us closer to the desired result or further away from the desired result.

"When the process is refined to the point that it is proven beyond a logical doubt to produce the desired result, and that desired result is proven to benefit individuals, a standard can then be agreed upon. At that point it is beginning to be obvious to many people where great results are occurring, and those who are achieving great results can easily explain why it is so.

"Allow me to reiterate, however, that the determination of a specific result one desires in the future and the process that yields that desired result are two totally different components of what is actually necessary to achieve the desired result. Expecting to reach some lofty goal without a process in place to get one there is wishful thinking. Similarly, creating a process that gives everyone something to do without any thought or decision about a specific end result is a complete waste of time and resources."

Christy raised her hand. "Again, with my husband," she said. "He works with so many teenagers. Brady is in the high schools all the time, and we have had long discussions about what he sees. Occasionally he will suggest or even require a change in the way a kid dresses or a particular piece of jewelry worn. One of the things he hears from parents is that this or that is a cultural thing. They say, 'We do this because it's part of our culture.' How in the world do you change something so ingrained?"

Jones nodded. "Good question. That culture, remember—any culture—is a result of the thinking that created it. Good thinking to great results yields a good culture. Bad thinking usually creates the opposite. We must remember to ask parents the question, 'What result do you want for your children when they become adults?' It is also a good question for a teenager.

"Many different groups of younger people wear specific clothes and wear them in a specific manner in order to be recognized as belonging to something in one form or another. But it is important to trace a culture's trajectory. What results are produced by twenty-five-year-old adults who participated as teenagers in a culture that accepted facial piercings as part of a normal appearance? Are those twenty-five-year-olds hired at the same rate as twenty-five-year-old adults who were immersed in a teenage culture promoting khaki pants, button-down shirts, and carefully groomed hair?

"What are the differences in their relationship results? What are the differences in their incomes at age thirty? What are the results being achieved by their own children?"

We were quiet as Jones stopped and seemed to be gauging the group's reaction. "Look," he finally said, "the example I just gave you is obviously a bit extreme. However, it is no less true. Everything a person does—whether parent or child—has consequences. One can easily follow dress, behavior, and habits to the result they produce.

"The bottom line on the declaration, 'This is part of our culture,' is this: At its best, this is a choice made with little or no critical thinking about future results. At its worst, it is merely an excuse to do what one wants to do. It is selfish, leaderless, pack behavior with unconsidered consequences that ultimately destroy families, neighborhoods, cities, and before you know it, generations.

"Always remember that your family has a culture, your team has a culture, and your town and your state have cultures too. Dallas has a culture, and it is a different culture than the one you will find in Fort Worth. America has a culture. Every culture is nothing more than a result of the thinking that produced it. A culture is chosen by its people, either by deliberate decisions or acquiescence to how everyone feels at the time.

"The culture you live in today is the culture you have allowed. That is true of your family, and it is true of your country.

"Never forget that you will shape the culture in which you exist, or the culture you allow will determine how and—maybe someday—*if* you are allowed to exist."

No one said a word. Polly took my hand. Jones didn't smile or frown. He looked at the sky for a time and leaned back against the pier railing. Personally, I didn't know if I wanted to stand up and cheer or crawl away and be sick. It all seemed so overwhelming. *How,* I wondered, *can we possibly begin to turn our cities? Where could we begin moving toward another golden age, another greatest generation?* I looked at the others. Were they asking themselves the same questions?

"Start at home," Jones said simply. I was not surprised that he answered my thoughts again. "Start with yourselves, with your families, with your children. The results you produce will be obvious and coveted by good folks everywhere. Those results will lead you and many of your friends to a process. That process will be refined by even greater results, and those results, proven in the lives of thousands—then tens of thousands—will yield a standard. Having been misunderstood and lost once upon a difficult time, that standard will be polished and protected and held up for all to see.

"Then you will see people of all colors and creeds come together in friendship and abundance. And it all will have started," Jones said with a smile, "with you.

"Anything else before we depart?" the old man asked.

"Are we meeting next week?" Christy responded.

Jones smiled. "I'm honored you seem to want to, but no, I don't think so. It is not my place to carry you all the way to a destination. I simply shine a bit of light on the path from time to time. But I'll be around. I always am."

We lingered for a time and exchanged phone numbers and e-mail addresses. Jones stayed for hugs and handshakes. I hugged but didn't question him about a "next time." I knew better, and of course, the question had already been asked. I had heard it answered that evening, I had heard it answered before, and he didn't need to tell me again. I could hear the old man's voice in my head anytime I wanted, for his answer was safely tucked away inside my heart.

"I'll be around. I always am."

That's what the man said. It felt good to know that it was true.

Seventeen

It was 2:51 a.m. when Christy rounded the curve on County Road 49. Less than an hour ago, Jones had called and asked her to pick him up on the north side of the bridge.

"Okay . . . ," Christy had said, buying time to think. "Jones, are you hurt? Where are you?"

"I'm fine. I'm at the Magnolia Springs River Bridge on County Road 49. I need you to come right away. And I need you to bring your little bus. Don't drive too fast. Be careful. Just come on. Brady will understand, and he will take care of the kids."

The headlights illuminated Jones's snow-white hair, and she spotted him immediately. He was sitting on the north end of the bridge, on the west-side guardrail. Fog, not yet high enough from the river to be a problem on the road, bumped softly under him as if he were seated on a cloud. To her photographer's eye, it was a fascinating sight, but another one in a long list, she thought, that would be gone in a minute or two and lost forever.

Christy was frustrated by scenes like this because she did not own the camera that would allow her to shoot natural light as it appeared in her mind. She and Brady had a game they would play when she saw something incredible that everyone else overlooked

175

completely. Christy would say, "I'd have that camera right now if it weren't for one tiny detail."

Brady would respond, "No money?"

"Yep, that's the detail," Christy would finish as they both laughed.

As Christy downshifted, she saw someone else with Jones. No, she decided, there were two people. As she drew closer, the weak, slightly yellow headlight beams illuminated those people, who had by now turned toward her, and Christy was surprised to see Sealy and Baker. Christy was baffled by the appearance of the other couple. *I thought he needed help.*

As she pulled the little bus onto the bridge, Christy's naturally enthusiastic nature began to wake up. No matter the time, she could not resist beeping the horn. Just as she always did, Christy gave the steering wheel two quick jabs, and the curious little vehicle responded. She did not notice Baker's scowl at having been almost scared into the water. Christy jumped out and said, "Is that horn cute or what? It sounds just like the Road Runner. Remember? In the cartoon?"

Yes, they remembered. Yes, it was cute. *It is also three o'clock in the morning*, Sealy thought and then wondered, *What in the world are we doing? I didn't even do things like this in college.*

Jones had called and awakened the Larsons only half an hour ago. They were already so grateful to him that neither of them even questioned his strange request for a meeting. They found flashlights as the old man had instructed, piled in one of the cars, and had come straight to the bridge. Jones showed Baker where to park, and the only thing he said was that Christy would arrive shortly and that they would all be back home "before too long."

"Everybody in," Jones said and clapped his hands. "Come on, now. Christy, let's turn this Road Runner around. We are headed back the way you came."

Sealy and Baker piled in through the side door. Christy climbed back into the driver's seat and waited for Jones to hop in the other side. He had briefly disappeared down the embankment and under the edge of the bridge. Arriving back at the bus, Jones rapped his knuckles on the side door that had already been shut. When Baker opened it, Jones shoved something big into his hands.

"Throw that in the back, please," Jones said, and Baker did, noticing that whatever it was felt awfully rough, but it was springy and about the size of a full garbage bag. "And these, too, please," Jones added. "You might need to run them under your legs and feet to get them to fit." Christy heard groans from Baker and laughter from Sealy as three long sticks were loaded in the dark. Baker couldn't really see what they were. Lighter and a bit longer maybe, he thought, but about as big around as a pool cue.

"Last thing," Jones said, and Baker took the object and placed it behind him. It was a medium-sized, canvas duffel. Its surface was smooth, and the handle was a single strap. *This thing*, Baker thought, *is as old as Jones*. He had also noticed it was rather light. In fact, Baker thought the duffel was empty. Until something inside clanked.

When they were on their way, by the time Christy had gotten back to Highway 98 and taken a left, Jones had already answered their most urgent questions. The answers were: (1) "Not going to tell you," (2) "About thirty minutes," and (3) "Onions."

The third answer was in response to giggles from the ladies when Baker had asked, "What's that smell?"

The big springy item Baker had thrown in the back, Jones explained, was an extra-large onion sack filled with more extra-large onion sacks. When they asked why in the world anyone might need onion sacks at three o'clock in the morning, Jones referred them back to answer number one.

"Since we're thirty minutes away from wherever we are going," Baker said, "do you mind if we ask some questions? We've been talking at the apartment and are curious about a few things."

"Sure," Jones replied. "I don't mind."

"I'm first!" Sealy shouted, prompting laughter from Christy since it was so out of character for Sealy to react that way.

"*Please* talk more about your reference to proper thinking," Sealy began. "Do you mind? It seems to be at the root of everything important, and Baker and I have the girls—teenagers, you know—and we feel like we need to explain the whole correct-thinking concept to them."

"I will," Jones said. "And you're right. The more you explain the concept, the clearer it will become to all of you. And at that point the implementation and agreement in your family about behaviors—ultimately a standard—based on great thinking will lead to harmony and higher levels of achievement."

"Will you do another class?" Sealy asked bluntly.

Jones chuckled appreciatively. "Sealy, I'm honored that you have found value in our time together, but a large part of the reason for ending the class is to enable you to learn and grow at a much faster rate than you have been doing lately."

"Wait. I know this is Sealy's question," Christy said, "but what does that mean? I have grown and learned more in the past two weeks than . . . well, than ever."

Baker agreed, but Jones did not back down. "Many times a person comes to rely on a specific teacher or class they've come to enjoy or appreciate. That often slows their progress, though few ever recognize the negative aspects of falling in love with something that works."

"How can there be a negative aspect of doing what you find that works?" Baker asked.

"Well," Jones said, "think of it like this: When a kid goes on his first Easter egg hunt, an adult has to take him by the hand. At this particular activity the adult is a skilled and knowledgeable instructor and teaches the grateful child exactly what to look for and how colored eggs are hidden.

"The child is being engaged in a process that is *already* paying big dividends. He has found something that works. *Why would I change anything?* he might ask, and that question to him, from his perspective, seems entirely reasonable. After all, just look at the eggs in his basket!

"However, that is exactly when a wise teacher pulls away. Why? For the greater benefit of the student. Certainly a teacher could acquiesce and agree to take the child by the hand until all the eggs have been found. But a *wise* teacher understands that the child who runs free—without the constraint of even the wisest teacher—can now achieve greater success by himself. The child has more energy than the teacher, a greater interest in colored eggs than the teacher, and more desire to run for hours than the teacher could ever hope to muster, fueled by the possibility of the ultimate prize—a golden egg.

"You may feel the class was incomplete . . . to which I would reply, 'Of course it was!' When a teacher covers every aspect of the subject, it can serve to exhaust the student, dampening what might have been an enthusiastic effort to learn more. Sadly, that most often ends the likelihood of that student experiencing the purest form of learning."

"Okay, I'll ask," Baker said. "What is the purest form of learning?"

"Learning's purest form," Jones replied, "is realized by the individual who continues a quest beyond the classroom, fueled by a passion to discern wisdom. Wisdom—genuine truth—holds the key to refining one's thinking.

"You see, in our particular class on parenting, the most

crucial achievement was the results list because those twenty-one outcomes clearly display the combined target for which your quest beyond our classroom must aim. If you will consult that list and use it to form your thinking as parents, you will produce seeds of wisdom that not only will bear fruit in the lives of your families but also will be sown into the hearts and minds of others.

"One seed, carefully tended, contains within it the power to change the world, for that single seed can yield an uncountable and ever-increasing number of seeds just as valuable.

"On the other hand," Jones added wryly, "if you were to continue waiting for Thursday evenings to roll around in order to hear what an old man thinks about parenting, you might be wandering through that material long after your children have grown up and moved away."

"Could you go back to the topic of correct thinking, please?" Sealy asked.

"I haven't forgotten." Jones looked at the road ahead to determine their location before speaking. "The way a person thinks," he began, "is the key to everything that follows, good or bad, success or failure. A person's thinking—the way he thinks—is the foundational structure upon which a life is built. Thinking guides decisions. Thinking—how a person thinks—determines every choice.

"Choices and decisions create action. Action is what a person does or says. Action is *when* a thing is done *and* how well or how often it's done. Action is what a person *says* and *to whom* and with what *tone of voice*. Action, in this sense, covers almost everything, except blinking and breathing. Even sleeping, for most, is an action that is chosen."

There were no comments, and Christy appeared to be wide-awake at the steering wheel, so Jones continued. "Actions, without exception, lead to results. A person's actions lead to good results, bad results, and no results. And don't forget that 'nothing' is an actual result. The thinking that chooses nothing as an action leads to a result of . . . say it with me . . ."

"Nothing!" they all said loudly, and Jones marveled at the energy and enthusiasm they were maintaining even in the middle of the night.

"All right," he continued. "Results manage to move beyond a person's physical presence. They never disappear but pile up and drift like a cloud, forming an invisible ring around a person. Incidentally, this results ring works the same way for a company or a family or a team. The ring can be magnetic and inviting and attracting. Or the ring can act as a fence or a wall, a barrier. We have a name for that ring. It's called a reputation.

"Some people and companies have rings around them—reputations—that attract opportunity. Others have rings around them—reputations—that repel opportunity. A single result rarely creates a reputation, whether that reputation is a good one or a bad one. Most invisible rings—reputations—are established over time by repetition.

"Interestingly, neither government regulation nor the lure of sympathetic feelings can circumvent natural law by forcing success into a life surrounded by a ring of squandered reputation. Success can be pulled but never pushed. Success can be attracted and received. It cannot be demanded or forced.

"Neither is a person able to skip part of the process. After *actions* that *result* in scandal or loss, a person may declare himself a different man and even change what he does for a time. But if his foundation has not been repaired . . . if his *thinking* has not been changed, the *results* produced by *actions* that have been determined by *choice* will inevitably show up again. A person's *thinking* is what he is. There's no getting around it.

"You might ask, 'Well, why doesn't that person get more

chances?' Until that person understands wisdom to a degree that his thinking is truly changed, he is not likely to be offered great opportunity." Jones paused to say, "Now, I'm not discussing whether someone deserves another chance. I am merely explaining why it is tougher to get a third chance or a fourth and so on, okay?"

They all indicated they understood, and Jones continued. "Here's the reason: by the time a bad reputation is in place, people who are in positions to offer this person another opportunity are well aware of the quality of *thinking* that made foolish *choices*, leading to unacceptable *actions*, which created the lousy *results* that established the bad *reputation* in the first place.

"Stay with me now . . . People who are in positions to offer an opportunity to someone else are usually in those positions because of their solid *reputations*—created by the excellent *results*, consistently achieved, due to productive *actions* that were set in motion by wise *choices* made possible by good *thinking*.

"And here is where it gets really interesting. People who are poised to provide opportunities for others obviously achieved that level of influence because of good thinking, right? Well, a crucial part of good *thinking*—certainly the kind of thinking you want to develop in your children—is the wise *choice* not to associate with a person who has taken the time to develop a bad *reputation* in the first place."

Jones peered down the road. "Christy, you'll need to make the left up here on 32. Hey, finishing on this topic, I cringe every time I hear somebody say, 'Everything happens for a reason.'"

"Why's that?" Baker asked.

"Oh, it's true enough, I suppose," Jones said with a sigh. "It's just that sometimes, the *reason* a thing happens is because that person's *thinking* was out of whack, and he made a stupid *choice*!"

Everyone laughed loudly, but Jones shushed them with a few

questions of his own. "Christy? How close are you financially to getting the camera you need?"

"I have some saved," she said. "I'm eighteen hundred dollars away, though. Not close enough."

Baker whistled. "That's some camera," he said.

"The one Christy will be getting," Jones said to him, "is the Kamado Joe of the photographic world."

"Gotcha!" Baker said. "I totally understand. You want the best. I've got to come up with some way to get those BigJoes and build my catering trailer."

"How much?" Jones asked.

"Twenty-five hundred, roughly," he said and turned to Sealy. "We need to do something fast for you, though." Back to Jones, Baker explained, "Sealy needs about fifteen hundred just to get started on the flower beds she contracted. We're in a tight spot, but I'll sell something, I guess. It just might have to be our clothes." Nobody responded, so Baker added, "That was supposed to be a joke, but it isn't funny to me either."

They were tired, and the laughter wasn't coming as easily. "Right here, Christy," Jones said. "This is County Road 3. Next is a left on Battles Road."

"Where are we?" Sealy asked, with no response. "Nobody knows?" There was still no response. Trying the direct approach, Sealy asked, "Jones, do *you* know where we are?"

"Yes ma'am, I do," he said, but offered no more.

"That's good enough for me," Sealy said, yawning. "Whoa . . . keep me awake, people. What should we talk about now? Jones?"

The old man didn't answer but looked down the road and up at the sky. "Time is getting short," he said.

No one was sure what he meant, and they were tired, so for the moment all was quiet in the little van. The tires hummed, and the light frame rattled. The three were silent, thoughts drifting to their families and the futures of their children. Softly, Jones said, "Battles Road, Christy. Left here."

As Christy made the turn, Jones added, "Next turn is fairly soon. You'll take a left on Twin Beech Road." Still, no one spoke. Christy was driving much slower. When they turned onto Twin Beech, they saw houses close to the street. Very few lights were on in the homes, but an occasional streetlight revealed a less prosperous neighborhood than existed in much of Baldwin County, and that included the tiny apartment where Baker and Sealy currently lived.

Wow! Baker thought. *I didn't even know this neighborhood was here and this is . . . what . . . maybe fifteen minutes from where we live? I will not gripe about a nine-hundred-square-foot apartment anymore.*

Baker continued to watch as they passed house after house with collapsing foundations or the soft beams of a nightlight or clock shining through cracks between boards. *Holes in the walls to the outside . . . How do they heat that place? Or cool it?* he wondered. *Maybe they just don't. Whew! I'm realigning my thinking right now,* Baker determined to himself. Then he had another thought. *I hope Sealy is seeing this. We are not cursed. We are blessed . . . we are fortunate. Okay, Baker Boy. There's your new perspective: your family gets to live in a luxury apartment. Please, God, make sure I remember this . . .*

"Right here, Christy," Jones said softly. "Park under the big oak."

As the van turned off the road, its weak headlights illuminated an oak with branches extending almost to the ground. Living in the area, they also recognized the sound of oyster shells crackling and popping under the tires. It wasn't as common as it had been decades before, but there were still some old driveways and wooded lanes "paved" in shells that had been shucked and discarded.

The van creaked to a stop at about the same time Christy's hand flew to her mouth. Sealy gasped, and Baker, straining to see around Jones, exclaimed, "What the . . ." and allowed the rest to go unsaid. Jones chuckled softly and opened his door. The others did not follow him, their eyes and imaginations focusing on a once-white board hanging crookedly from one of the oak's branches. The yellowish headlights cast odd shadows past the board, revealing more than any of them wanted to see.

Jones was outside the van and tapped on the window, causing them all to jump. "Come on," he said quietly. "Let's go."

"No thanks," Christy said. "Really. I'm fine."

Not one of them moved. But they did look at the board again. It was swinging gently in the breeze. *Twin Beech Cemetery*, it read. *Established 1817.*

Eighteen

Baker and Sealy scrambled out of the vehicle. Christy remained inside. "Go ahead," she told them. "I'll be *right here.*" It was a standoff.

After a moment's hesitation Jones said, "Okay then. We should be back in a couple of hours." With the duffel bag in his right hand, the onion sacks under his right arm, and the sticks under his left, the old man moved to step through the gate of a white picket fence. Reluctantly Baker and Sealy turned to follow.

"Oh no you don't!" Christy said as she scrambled from the bus. "You are not going to leave *me* here." With as much indignation as she could produce, Christy slammed the side door, mumbling, "This is crazy." She sailed past the Larsons and, with her flip-flops clicking indignantly, marched directly to Jones. "May I have a stick, please?" she requested.

Without a word Jones handed her a stick. Christy hit the ground with it a couple of times, feeling its heft before jabbing at an oak tree and crying, "Ha!" At that, the group was trying hard not to laugh. Sealy snorted as Christy said to Jones, "I am ready. Lead on, Jones." She brandished the stick at the group and added, "I will pop a ghost in the head with this. You people had *best* stay close to me."

They were so tired they could barely see straight and were laughing so hard they could barely walk. But with flashlights, one gas lantern, an old man leading, and guarded by a woman with a stick, the four managed to get across Twin Beech Cemetery without incident.

Jones had taken them to the far end of the small graveyard. They were laughing as they gathered around the old man. More than once Christy had lunged at nothing with her stick, saying, "Ha!" She always followed that action with a stream of encouragement and commentary. "You guys are safe," she would say. "You're doing good. Just keep walking. *Keeeep* walking. Everybody's fine. Doing real good. Almost across now, and may I say that you people are lucky to have me with you. Baker, let me know if I need to fight a zombie or something. Don't be afraid, buddy. I have your back."

They stopped at a break in the fence, and Jones passed a stick to Baker and Sealy. Baker had offered to carry the onion sacks or the duffel or something, but the old man had declined. Now Baker was examining a stick by the glow of the flashlight. It was stout bamboo, cured and unyielding. The women, however, were looking toward the dense wooded area beyond the cemetery.

Suddenly Christy ditched the humor. "Are we going *that* way?" she asked.

"Yes," Jones said with a smile. "And it will be a worthwhile journey. Follow me," he said as he stepped into the woods.

"Jones, wait," Christy pleaded. Then in a louder voice, because he had not waited and was in fact moving away, she asked, "What are the sticks for?"

The old man didn't stop but threw a "You'll see" over his shoulder before adding, "Don't lose it, though. For now, use it to hit the ground in front of you as you walk. That'll make the snakes get out of your way."

Sealy glanced at Christy, whose only reaction was a shudder. As they followed along in the dark, Christy didn't say another word. Baker thought that was funny. *She really is scared now*, he decided.

It was only minutes before their tight group began to spread out a bit. Jones was setting a fast pace. There was mud, water, and thick stands of brush and needle grass. Fallen pine trees—remnants from hurricanes and tropical storms—were strewn like a vast Tinkertoy maze, blocking every turn they made. Worst of all, snakes really did appear to be a threat. Certainly water moccasins were on their minds as they made their way over and through swampy terrain like none of them had ever experienced.

There were massive, unchecked vines laced with razor-sharp thorns. They were up the trees, across bushes, and growing along the ground. Everyone was cut in several places, and Sealy had received a particularly nasty gash under her left eye. Christy's feet were bleeding, prompting Sealy to put an arm around her waist as they navigated a patch of needle grass. Christy's flip-flops were not holding up well.

They were all having a hard time keeping up with the old man, who seemed oblivious to their difficulties. He was becoming difficult to see. It was dark, of course, and his light was directed forward, away from the group. "Not much time," they heard him say from up ahead. "Don't stop." None of them had liked this from the beginning. Now, however, they were annoyed, well on the way to becoming angry.

Christy was climbing over the trunk of a tree when Baker yelled. He had stepped into a hole and turned his ankle. *Badly*, she thought, if the look on his face was any indication. The hole had been covered with grass and brush and had been virtually undetectable. She was the only one close enough to help. Sealy was ahead, Christy thought, but figured she would come back to help her husband.

Christy was already exhausted, and by the time she got Baker to his feet, she was dizzy too. Now, apparently, he would need to lean on her to get out of here. *Where is Sealy?* she wondered. She couldn't see any light but her own lantern. Not Sealy's. Not Jones's.

Baker decided he couldn't walk and eased himself back down. Trying hard not to cry, Christy joined Baker on the ground and burst into tears anyway. She was muddy, bleeding, and exhausted in every sense of the word.

When Baker began calling her name, Sealy converged on the sound, finally found them, and leaned, breathing hard, against a tree. At that moment, if anyone had told them they had left the cemetery only twenty-three minutes before, none of them would have believed it. "Where is Jones?" Sealy asked.

Baker shook his head. He did not have any clue as to the old man's whereabouts and had not for a while. Less than a hundred yards in, Baker had tangled his arm in razor thorns. The deep scratches were obviously not his only wounds, merely the first, but he had not seen Jones after that. Baker was attempting to control his rising anger, but he was about to be past trying.

"Did he leave us here?" Christy cried. "I am so stupid. I never should have done this."

"Which way is back?" Sealy asked. "I'm so turned around . . ."

Baker pointed to his right. "That way. There's been an east wind for two days. It was at our backs when we left the cemetery."

"Do you think Jones is lost?" Christy asked.

"No," Baker said. "No, I don't."

"You are correct," came a voice from the darkness. And when they looked, Jones was less than ten feet from them. His flashlight must have been in his pocket because the old man was very close, yet they had not seen him. There were general comments from the three, but it was not a joyful welcome. They were relieved he was there, but they weren't certain if they were happy with him.

"How long have you been here?" Sealy demanded. "How long have you been standing right here?"

"The whole time," Jones admitted.

"That's not true," Christy said accusingly. "You left us alone out here."

"No, I didn't," Jones replied. "I was around. I always am."

"That's the same thing you said to me the other night," Christy noted.

"You're right," Jones said to Christy. "It is exactly what I said to you the other night."

Jones waited for anyone else to speak up. When no one did, he brushed off a place on the ground, eased to one knee, and asked, "So . . . what are you going to do?" There was still no response. "Maybe now's the time to quit and go back the way you came. You know for sure what's behind you. It can't be any worse . . .

"On the other hand, you have no clue what lies ahead." He cocked his head and smiled mysteriously. "And it could get *a lot* worse. Truly, you don't know whether this thorny chaos will last five more minutes or five more hours."

He stood up and addressed the three of them. "As I said, you were never alone. In fact, my eyes have been on you at every moment. Less than thirty minutes ago, when this particular part of your journey began, you were close enough to me that, had you asked, I would have held your hand or even carried you.

"At the beginning I asked you to do one thing. As you stepped into the unknown, I issued a single, very simple instruction.

That instruction, as casual and unimportant as it might have sounded to you only half an hour ago, continues even now to be the critical component that will determine your future, which begins with the success or failure of tonight's adventure."

Jones looked carefully at the three people before him. They were damaged and dirty, exhausted and wary, but he loved them even when they ignored him or rejected his efforts to help as they had done this evening. With a patient smile the old man simply explained the path they had chosen and the immediate results that choice had produced.

"Ignoring my instruction, your minds quite naturally drifted from the safety that wise counsel can provide. Of course, your physical actions quickly followed, and just that quickly"—Jones snapped his fingers—"you were in trouble.

"Darkness commands an inordinate amount of attention from a person who is unprepared and unprotected. Attention to darkness produces doubt. When a person is distracted and weakened by struggles, doubt whispers a message logically urging surrender; and soon, that person's focus is on his own discomfort, his fear and anger, regret and resentment.

"That is precisely what happened with you," Jones noted. "'Follow me,' I said. It was my only request. When you did not, the inevitable occurred, and you lost sight of me completely. To you, it seemed as though I were not there at all. Yet, even then, had you only stopped to call my name, I would have made my presence known, and your vision—your vision that sees even in the darkness—would have returned."

Without a glance away from them, Jones pointed in the direction of the bay. "For I know well the plans I have made for you," he said. "These are plans to prosper you—not to allow harm to come to you—but plans to give you hope and an incredible future."

Jones picked up his duffel bag. "So let's try this again, shall we? Follow me," he said and turned as if to go. Incredibly, still, the three hesitated, glancing nervously at each other.

"Where are we going?" Baker asked.

"Son," Jones said with a sigh, "if we leave right now, all will be well. But if you continue to question everything I say, you will not accomplish anything. Is it not enough that you know I would not get you up in in the middle of the night and bring you through all of this without some purpose?"

Baker was in pain. His wife was bleeding. Christy was in no better shape. "Jones . . . I just don't understand."

"Yes, I know that you don't," Jones replied, "but it's an odd thing you've been unable to grasp . . . See, I'm not requiring you to understand. I am simply urging you to obey. For it is only when you obey that, eventually, you begin to understand."

Jones gestured for them to come close. When they had gathered in a tight group, the old man pointed in the direction of the wind and spoke. "The bay is there. You did not know how close you were when you quit. There is still time. There is more difficult terrain to traverse. Yes, before you are out of this wilderness, you might stumble, and you may fall. But listen to me . . . you make it to that bay even if you have to crawl.

"Every step you take is a step of faith. If you can't see in front of you, walk on, and just believe. Don't despair. Whisper words of prayer. And when you get there . . ." Jones shook his head, laughing softly. Placing his arms around them, he squeezed and finished what he had been about to say. "When you get there, the miracle, I promise, will be waiting in the water."

With renewed determination, and only minor difficulties compared to what they had already experienced, the small group was out of the thick woods in only a few minutes and found themselves on a road. Stopping briefly to inspect each other with their flashlights, they were amazed to be walking around. "We look like escapees from a trauma unit," Sealy said. Then they hobbled as fast as they could toward Jones, whose flashlight they could see bobbing its way through a wooded lot.

When at last they reached the bay, Jones got down on his knees to open the bag. "Sticks, please," he said. "Just point them down here." By the light of Christy's lantern, Jones fastened a sharp spike of some sort on the end of each stick.

"Woohoo! I'll get a ghost for sure with this," Christy said. "I am looking dangerous now. Who are we fighting, Jones?"

The old man smiled and said only, "Turn them around, please. I need the other end." Out of the duffel came wire frames. Shaped in a circle except for one flat side, the frames were threaded with a small white net. Each attached snugly to the end of the stick that was opposite the spike.

"A net?" Baker said. "A net and a javelin. This is a very curious contraption for the middle of the night."

Jones closed the duffel bag and stood. "It's not the middle of the night anymore, Baker," he said. "It is four thirty-nine in the morning." Baker pushed the button on his watch that illuminated the digital numbers. It was, he saw, 4:39 a.m. Jones emptied the onion sacks—bags of heavy plastic mesh—onto the ground. "Each of your names has been written on the labels of five sacks. Grab one of yours and tie it to your belt or onto a belt loop," he instructed. "The pile of extras will be here, but always be sure to use your own."

"Use it for what?" Sealy asked but received no answer.

"Jones," Christy said fearfully, "are we supposed to go *into* the water? I can't go in it, Jones. I just can't."

Jones responded, but his answer was directed to everyone. "Yes, I want everyone in the water. Go in now, please, and spread out. Allow thirty or forty feet between you. About knee-deep will be perfect, and carry your sticks and lights with you."

Jones drew Christy aside and placed his hands on her shoulders. She was trembling. "Look at me, Christy." She did, but the tears in her eyes made it hard to see. "Christy, you will be fine," Jones said. "The water will not be deeper than the middle of your thigh. To make sure you feel safe, however, I will ease out past where you are and keep you between myself and the shore." He gestured toward the Larsons, who were already wading in, and said, "Go."

Christy took several uncertain steps before stopping for a bit more reassurance. "And you'll be with me?" she asked. "Seriously? You'll be close?"

The old man smiled and nodded. "I always am," he said.

When all three were in the water, they waded around, looking at minnows or hermit crabs for several minutes, but they were exhausted, in pain, and soon tired of what little fun this was to begin with. Jones was beyond them in water almost to his chest. He did not have his light, but they knew where he was and, this time, kept him in sight.

The water was warm—almost hot—and the east wind had died to almost nothing. The surface of the bay looked like glass, the only ripples at all caused by three people standing in the dark with a spike and a net.

"Jones?"

"Yes, Christy?"

"My feet hurt."

"You'll be fine."

"Jones?" came another voice.

"You'll be okay too, Sealy."

"What are we doing out here?" Christy asked. "Brady is going to kill me. I have joined the crazy club. I am as crazy as—" and she screamed. Sort of . . .

The vocal oddity produced from the throat of the beautiful young woman at that moment was accomplished without the slightest pause for breath. In fact, her cry might have made the others laugh hysterically had it not unnerved them so completely.

The scream itself was less "classic shriek" than "weird, strangled exhalation of total surprise." Performed in midsentence, without the benefit of even the quickest breath taken to power its sound, in reality, the bizarre squeal was simply the resonate result of classic overreaction and would have been a more appropriate vocal choice to accompany the instant of one's grisly death.

"Christy! Are you all right?" came Sealy's voice.

Christy had high-stepped several feet away when she screamed, creating huge geysers of water. If they had been sure a shark had not attacked, it would have been funny. Christy was soaking wet, standing like a statue with her spear at the ready, illuminated by two shaky flashlights and her old gas lantern. Baker and Sealy were frozen, too, unsure whether to rescue their friend or run for their lives.

"Something hit my leg!" Christy said, still not moving.

Suddenly Sealy yelled and danced a quick circle. "There are things down there," she said, bending over with her light. "I see some things. They were on my foot. Oh my—they have glowing eyes! What are those things?"

The attention was evenly divided between Christy and Sealy until Baker jumped. "Okay, that was big. Jones? Whatcha got going here?" He heard the old man chuckle from somewhere in the dark.

Sealy was still looking down at her feet. "Christy! Come here! Bring your big light. I can see these things, but I can't see what they are." Hesitating, Christy moved toward Sealy, who was poking her net at whatever she was seeing. "I think it's—" Before she could finish her statement, one of whatever they were flicked across the top of the water and right into Sealy's net. "It's a shrimp!" she yelled. "Baker! I caught a shrimp. He's huge."

Christy had just made it to Sealy's side and shined the lantern, which was much brighter than the flashlights, into the net. "How cool," she said. "Oh, he *is* big."

"Christy, be still . . . Oh . . . Christy, look." Sealy grabbed Christy's hand that was holding the lantern and slowly swung the light away from the white net. Christy gasped. "The eyes are from shrimp," Sealy said. "Those are *all* shrimp!" She looked around for her husband and found him when she heard a splash.

"Guys!" Baker said. "Look at this!" Up and out of the water, into the air he swung the pointed end of his stick and hanging from it was a flounder the size of a dinner platter.

"What kind of fish is that?" Christy hollered to Baker. "Those are all around me."

"It's a flounder, Christy," Baker said. "Gig them!"

"What?" she responded. Christy wasn't sure whether she was horrified or not.

"Gig 'em, girl," Sealy said, brandishing her stick. "That's what the sharp end is for. It's a flounder gig. Goodness gracious, look at the fish!"

"It's a jubilee!" Baker yelled. "Look! Everything is headed to shore!"

It was, and they were. For about seventy yards of shoreline, right where they stood, the calm water was literally beginning to quiver. There were blue crabs and whiting mingled in, but most of what they saw at first were shrimp and flounder. Within five minutes the sea creatures were so thick around their legs that it was difficult to walk.

The flounder were stacking on top of each other, and Baker was often putting four and five at a time in the onion sack tied to his waist. Sealy and Christy were having no less success, and, in fact, it was Christy who dragged the first full sack onto the shore. She quickly tied another bag marked with her name onto a belt loop and hurried back into the water.

Sealy had developed her own technique for capturing the shrimp. She put the net straight down beside her feet and held the stick firmly with one hand at the top and the other down by the net. She walked forward slowly making the net drag on the bottom, and by the time she had moved six feet, the net would be full. Sealy was putting more than five pounds of shrimp at a time in her onion sack. Within twenty minutes, her first bag was tied off, filled with more shrimp than she could drag out of the water by herself.

As the jubilee started, Baker recognized what was happening and said to his wife and Christy, "This is a once-in-a-lifetime experience, ladies. Remember what you're seeing here, but work while it's happening. The seafood markets will buy everything we can get."

It was all the encouragement they needed. They saw stingrays, too sluggish to hurt anyone, and crabs with claws as big as chicken legs, lying in the shallows as if asleep. Huge schools of mullet, hundreds of fish at a time, swam slow circles around the top, kissing the surface of the water for the oxygen they were seeking. But it was the shrimp, layering the bottom like thick carpet, and the flounder in six inches of water, stacked like giant pancakes, that astounded them.

As dawn began to break, they worked faster. Even in the water they were hot and teased Jones about staying cool in the deeper water. They were intent on making the most of a situation whose end could come at any minute. There were twelve sacks full of shrimp and flounder stacked onshore when Jones said, "The tide is changing. Give it all you've got. This won't last much longer."

The morning light was increasing by the minute, and Christy was as tired as she had ever been in her life. When Baker staggered by to put another sack on the shore, he offered to take her gas lantern. At first she didn't understand, but he pointed with the gig to the flounder scattered around them and said, "Look. You don't need it. Let me put it with the bags."

He was right, and everyone quickly discarded their lights. Without the awkwardness of two hands doing three things, they were moving freely and much faster. When the jubilee had begun, they heard Baker say that the local seafood dealers would buy what was harvested, and they were all working with a purpose.

Sealy gathered the shrimp and flounder with Christy. Both women were thinking about their businesses and the possibility that this miracle from nowhere might fund their starts. They were not sure, however, exactly what this might be worth, and neither wanted to stop for a second to ask Baker if he knew.

It would not have mattered. Baker did not know either. He had fished all his life, but he had never sold any of what he had caught. It was always eaten right away, put in the freezer, or given to friends. Baker knew that seafood was expensive in restaurants, but how much anyone might pay for a flounder or a pound of shrimp fresh out of the water, he had not the faintest idea. As he put more flounder in the sack at his waist, however, Baker did think about those Kamado Joe grills and how nice they would look on his rolling kitchen.

Christy caught shrimp for what seemed like a long time to her and was now gigging flounder at a frantic pace. She thought about her camera and what she would be able to accomplish with it. While photographers were everywhere, Christy's talent was unique. Her photographs had already won awards, but Christy knew that there was only one camera that would produce the pictures she had in her mind . . . and that camera was expensive. How many fish could you trade for a camera? Christy did not know.

"Christy?" Jones called gently. "You need to move back in. Move toward shore a bit. Be sure to stay in shallower water, now especially. The current is picking up with this tide, and you don't want to be caught in it." To the others in a louder voice, he announced, "Everything is beginning to wake up. I think you have less than ten minutes to work. Push yourselves just a little longer!"

Christy thanked Jones for the warning and turned toward shore. Though the sun was not officially up, it was fully daylight, and everyone was doing as the old man suggested: what they could, while they could.

Within a short time the three were milling about, attempting to capture the last of what they could see. They were talking excitedly about how the sea creatures had now seemed to wake up, shake off their sluggishness, and hightail it for deeper water. To their additional amazement, they looked at the sacks piled up on the small beach, and all agreed they had not put a dent in the numbers of fish and shrimp that had been under their feet for the past hour and a half. To a person, they thought, it looked as if there were as much flounder and shrimp in the water at the end of the jubilee as when it started.

Sealy and Christy were finished. Having stuck their gigs in the sand, they stood in a foot of water near the shore, watching Baker, who was close by, continuing to prowl along, looking for one last flounder.

"Baker," Sealy called, "we voted, and you get to bring Christy's little bus to us."

"Okay," Baker said with his head down, "but I'm going around, not through . . . Even if it's around the world, I'm not fighting the Amazon jungle again to get that bus."

They laughed just as Baker made a mighty lunge with his gig. Looking up with a big grin, Baker said, "Missed him. Ha! That is the first one I've missed, but it's the first one I've seen swimming a hundred miles an hour! That's it, I think. They are awake and too fast for me."

Baker made it to the group in several big, splashing steps and gestured to the sacks of seafood. "Good grief!" he exclaimed. "I don't know how much we have, but I do need to get to the vehicle. We need to get this on ice or take it somewhere. Good grief," he said again. "What do we put the stuff in to ice it down? There aren't enough ice chests in Fairhope to hold all this."

Standing beside the sacks, Baker nudged Sealy and said, "Honey? Are you sure I should walk all the way to the bus? My ankle is—"

"Your ankle was fine when you were running all over the bay, gigging flounder a few minutes ago," Sealy said.

"Guys?"

They turned and saw Christy moving toward them. "What's wrong?" Baker asked.

"Jones is gone," she said looking around. "At least I . . . well, I guess he's gone. When he got out of the water, he sat down over there." Christy pointed. "He was right there."

They walked to the place Christy had last seen him and looked up and down the beach, but Jones was nowhere in sight. "He's probably gone to get Christy's bus," Baker said.

Christy pulled keys from her pocket. "No," she said. "He would have asked for the keys."

"Did he walk to town?" Sealy asked. "Maybe he went to get ice?"

"Well, no matter what," Baker said. "We have to get ice, and we'd better do it now." He stopped and looked hard at something down the shoreline from where they stood.

"Do you see him?" Sealy asked excitedly.

Baker looked at her. "No, honey," he said and fixed his gaze down the beach again. "Now that it's daylight, I think I know where we are." He pointed. "I am almost certain that's Jack Bailey's house. Listen, you two stay here. If you can, get some water on those bags of shrimp and flounder. I'll run and enlist Jack. Or at least use his phone."

Baker began to shuffle through the sand in the direction of the Baileys' house. He only went a hundred feet or so before he turned around and yelled, "Hey! Don't worry about Jones. He'll be back soon!"

Nineteen

I awaken early on most days, often well before dawn, but when my cell phone rang that Monday morning, I was still in bed. The phone was on a chair across the room, though, and I wasn't sure where it was located. In a dazed half-sleep I did not know how long it had been ringing and was not inclined to answer it anyway. I rolled over and waited for the noise to stop. When it did, I glanced at the clock. It was almost eight thirty.

The phone began ringing again. Why was I still in bed? Deeply fatigued and having just been forced into consciousness, my thoughts were muddled, but travel delays and a canceled flight soon came into focus. Stranded in Atlanta the night before, I had rented a car, driven the six hours to Orange Beach, and gotten to sleep just before five that morning.

I was alone. Evidently Polly had taken the boys to school and allowed me to sleep. The thought crossed my mind that I *still* would have been sleeping had I turned off my phone. It was now ringing for the third time. Finally, thankfully, it stopped . . . and almost immediately began ringing again.

I kicked the covers off a bit more aggressively than usual and lurched across the bedroom for the phone. Not recognizing the number displayed on the screen, I hesitated just long enough for it to stop ringing. Not trusting this mysteriously persistent marathon caller to give up, I waited, and, sure enough, it rang again.

Okay, okay, you win, I thought and grudgingly answered.

"Mr. Andrews?" a woman's voice asked.

Sorry. You first, I thought. "Who's calling, please?"

"This is Jack Bailey's assistant. Is this Mr. Andrews?"

Jack Bailey's assistant? What was this about? "Yes, it is," I answered.

She must have immediately handed the phone to Jack because his voice was the next I heard. "Andy?"

"Yes, Jack . . . how are you?"

"Oh, I'm fine, but our buddies are in a bit of a jam. I hope you don't mind, but I got your number from Sandy Stimpson."

This was strange. I had only met Jack a couple of times and barely knew him. "No problem," I said. "What's going on? Which buddies and what jam?"

After Jack gave me a brief rundown, I threw on some shorts and a T-shirt, wrote a quick note for Polly, and left the house.

A little less than an hour later, I was sitting on a driftwood log by myself, waiting for Jack Bailey. I was sure this was the place we were supposed to meet, but where was Jack?

Three people were bunched together far down the beach from where I continued to wait. They were too far away to recognize, but I was fairly certain it had to be the Larsons and Christy Haynes.

Hearing a voice behind me, I stood and saw Jack Bailey approaching, talking on his cell phone. Finishing the call about the time he reached me, Jack smiled and extended his hand. "I apologize for keeping you waiting."

We shook hands. "No problem." I saw his gaze move to the three down the beach. "Nothing happening that I can tell," I said, and he nodded.

"Our house is right down there," Jack pointed. "Seven . . . eight lots away . . . if you'd rather, we can head that way. We can watch them from the wharf."

"No . . . I'm fine," I said. "Thanks though. Maybe later?"

"Sure."

"So, Jack, I mean, seriously . . ." I held my hand up to my eyes, shading them as I looked again at the three figures slowly working their way toward us. I shook my head in amused disbelief and looked at the man who had wanted this meeting. "They really think something might be wrong?"

Jack grinned. "Do you remember the first time he disappeared on you?"

I spread my arms in an "Are you kidding?" gesture. "He always disappears! To this day I don't know if he's in town or not."

Jack smiled and nodded. "We'll calm them down when they get back." He motioned toward his house and said, "I see Mary Chandler on the end of our wharf. She's talking to someone on her cell, but it's not me." He held his phone out and grinned, making me smile too. "You sure you don't want to head to the house?"

"Thanks, but I'm comfortable," I said, as though I were back at the Grand Hotel in a suite. As if to prove how pleasant it was, I sat back down on the log. After a moment Jack joined me. We both looked at the three. They were steadily getting closer. Without taking my eyes from them, I grinned and asked, "Which one of them thought he might have drowned?"

"Christy," he said. "By the time Baker and I got back here, she and Sealy had already called 911 at one of my neighbors' houses. You know Hoss Mack . . ." I nodded, acknowledging that

I did know the popular sheriff. "Well," Jack continued, "I called Hoss right away. Thankfully I got him before they launched the flotilla."

Both of us were laughing at that point. "Good grief," I said. "You *know* the old man would have shown up if they had started dragging the bay for his body. He never would've been able to resist it."

Jack grabbed my arm. "He probably would've floated up by one of the boats, and when they bent over to get him, would have rolled over and said hello!" We fell over in the sand then, laughing until we couldn't. It was an unusual bond between Jack and me—having the old man in common—and I think we both enjoyed that moment in a way no one else could have.

"You know, Jack," I said as I attempted to stretch my back, "I have always wondered why, here on the Eastern Shore, you all call them 'wharves.' Like, 'This is my wharf,' or 'Look at the wharf' . . ."

"What do you call them?" Jack asked.

"Docks. We say, 'Meet me on the dock,' or 'They did a nice job on that dock.' Here, you call it a wharf. In Orange Beach, it's a dock. And we're only forty-five minutes away from each other. Same state. Same county, even."

"I never thought of that," Jack said and looked at our friends who were getting closer and closer. "Wait until you see them up close. They look like they've been through a war."

I frowned. "What do you mean?"

Jack looked at me. "Oh . . . sorry. I forgot you didn't know." He turned around and motioned toward the road and the woods beyond. "Sometime in the middle of the night, the old man led them through there. They came from the old cemetery and got through *that* in the dark." He paused as if trying to capture a thought that had fluttered by his consciousness for a moment, only to dance away, out of reach. "I've been in there in the daylight and thought I'd never get out. They are scratched and cut to pieces."

I didn't understand. "Why would he bring them through there?"

Jack looked at me with an odd expression. "For the jubilee," he said.

I was frowning. None of this made any sense at all. "Jack, have you ever even witnessed a jubilee?" He shook his head no. "No," I said, "and neither have I or my wife or any of our friends. *You* haven't seen one, and you live on the shore where they take place!

"Now, how in the heck did these guys come through here in the middle of the night and just happen upon one?" I glanced around. "And I guess they managed to get some flounder. You can smell the fish. There's shrimp over there on the ground, so they must have spilled a few from some bucket they picked up somewhere. I just don't get it. How is it possible for anybody to happen upon a jubilee? What are the odds?"

When I paused, Jack had tilted his head to the side and looked at me through narrowed eyes. "They didn't happen upon it."

"What?"

"He sent them into the water, had them spread out . . ." Jack stopped again.

"Oh, come on," I scoffed, a hint of aggravation beginning to appear. "He had them spread out? He had them spread out and what?"

"This is what they told me," Jack said coolly. "Apparently the old man spread them out, and five minutes after they were in the water, a jubilee happened around them."

Jack smiled and reached into his back pocket, retrieving an oversized brown envelope. His eyes twinkled like Jones's as he removed what was obviously folded paper. I smiled, seeing an expression on Jack's face one doesn't often see on an adult. But I recognized it. His countenance was that of a sixth grader some-one had just called a liar. Now that kid had assembled everyone on the playground and was about to prove that what he had said was true.

He held the paper up for me to see and twisted it between his thumb and first two fingers. The paper—papers—spread in the way playing cards do. Whatever Jack Bailey held in his hand, I now saw there were three. But three what?

He continued to hold the papers but placed his hand behind his back and seemed to change the subject. "They had onion sacks," Jack said. Opening his eyes wide, he added, "They had a lot of onion sacks. They didn't have a bucket, Andy. When the old man spread them out, they had onion sacks with their names on the labels. They each had a gig, a net, and a light. They were in the water before it happened. They were prepared."

Jack walked me over to a flattened area of grass. "This is where the pickups came in to haul the sacks out of here. Those shrimp on the ground just fell out of holes in the sacks." He was watching me carefully and beginning to get that cocky look the sixth grader has after he has proven his point.

"I just . . . It's a bit much, isn't it? Even for you and me, I mean. And we know . . . Well, it's astounding and typical all at the same time." I was still trying to process the evidence in front of me.

"You know Carson Kimbrough, right? Big seafood dealer?" Jack asked.

I nodded. "Very well. Awesome guy. In fact, Carson and Cynde live around the corner from us."

"Well, I called Carson. He sent a refrigerated truck and a guy with scales and a checkbook. They took all fourteen bags."

"You sold it all?" I asked in amazement.

"Yes, I sold it," Jack said, laughing. "What did you think

we were going to do with it? Clean and put it in Ziploc bags in the freezer? It was more than six hundred pounds of shrimp and almost nine hundred pounds of flounder."

My jaw had fallen somewhere around my knees. It was still almost beyond comprehension. "Yeah," Jack said, seeing my reaction. "Yeah, I am telling you, I have never seen that much fish and shrimp in one place in my life! Here . . . look."

From behind his back he produced the three papers and handed them to me. "The bags had names on them," Jack said. "I had Carson's guy weigh them separately and write the checks according to what names were on which bags. See . . ." He gestured at the checks as I opened the envelope. "They're only first names, but it's a local bank, and if need be, Carson can add the last names before they cash them."

Again, I was stunned. "How much did you get for all that?"

"I just told him to do the best he could on the going rate," Jack said. "The flounder were whole, so he paid $2.50 a pound on them and the shrimp were huge. So $6.25 a pound there. I guess that's okay . . ."

"They are going to faint," I said. "You did a good thing here, Jack. These folks need this." I went through the checks again before handing over the envelope. I had started to do the math in my head when Jack had told me the weights and per pound price—I just wanted to have some idea—but I realized the total was all separated nicely right in my hands.

Christy's check was for $1,824.50. Baker's check was a big one for $2,512.50, and his wife, Sealy, had earned $1,505. I was sure they would be happy, but I also knew that all three were being squeezed financially and hoped it would be what they needed.

My thoughts drifted to the old man. Once again I was amazed at what happened once he began to impart his guidance and perspective. "You know, Jack, Jones told me once that wisdom could not be diminished. He said, 'It can be silenced, it can be ignored, but it cannot be diminished. Wisdom will grow,' he said, 'as you seek it and add it into your life, but if you really want to see wisdom flourish . . . if you desire to see wisdom grow and bloom . . . you must plant a seed of it into the life of another.'"

Jack thought about that before nodding slowly. "Another seed reference," he remarked. "Once, long ago, I heard him say that he planted seeds often and generously, but those seeds only grew to full maturity in soil that was being tended diligently." Lifting his head and turning to look directly at me, Jack said, "There are so many things I'd like to know about him. Where does he go? Why doesn't he stay?" He glanced at me and said wryly, "Where is he right now?"

"According to him," I shrugged, "he's always around."

"I believe it," Jack said.

"I do too," I said. "In fact, I count on it."

We stood then and greeted Baker, Sealy, and Christy, who had finally arrived at our spot on the shore. They didn't appear to be incredibly tired, considering what they had experienced. Baker, in particular, looked remarkably buoyant. Jack noticed the same thing, shooting a questioning glance at me that seemed to ask, *What's up with Baker?*

As we talked, I grew ever more curious about Baker. Sealy and Christy, it appeared, were also somewhat baffled by his behavior. Baker did not act tired in the least. Quite the opposite, in fact, was the case. He was a bit over the top, almost euphoric, and I wasn't sure how to interpret his mood.

Jack gave them the checks, and it was awesome to be there to watch. Christy wept with joy, and pretty soon we had all joined the celebration with tears of our own. The three of them told us the story of what had happened in the middle of the night, before dawn, prompting each other, laughing and marveling at specific moments they remembered and would remember forever.

Jack asked if they were convinced about Jones's safety, and they assured us they were. In turn, we affirmed that they were correct in that assessment. Jones would return, we told them.

"Yep," Jack said, "trust me. It might be a decade before you see him again. Then again, the old guy could be taking a nap in your backseat this afternoon when you climb into your car. When will he be back? Where will he show up? Who knows? But count on this: you will see him again."

I agreed. "He's around," I added, "and, yes, he's fine." With that, Jack and I looked at each other and gave a little nod. Together we had verbally tied the situation up with a neat bow. I thought Jack had been articulate, and with my little postscript we were able to reach a logical end point for us all. It was the perfect time for everyone to shake hands, wish each other well, and say good-bye. We were about to do just that when Baker felt the need to agree with us.

"Oh, yeah," he said with a big smile. "He is fine. Yes! Jones is fine. He is better than fine. He is great. This is unbelievable, and I'm so happy. I have never been so . . . Well, I'm just so happy that he's fine. And he is fine. Absolutely fine. Great. Yes!"

Then he laughed.

It was one of the strangest things I have ever seen in my life. Jack and I exchanged a long look as Baker laughed. Christy's mouth was open, and her eyebrows were so high they threatened to merge with her hairline. We all looked at Sealy, who had not taken her eyes off her husband. It was as though she wanted to ask if he had taken something, but knowing he had not, she didn't bother. But it was apparent she was as mystified by her husband's behavior as the rest of us.

Baker's mood seemed transcendent—over the top—even more so than might be expected at such a moment.

I just didn't fully know why.

It had happened, it was over, and if what he had witnessed had lasted any less than the couple of minutes it did, Baker might not have believed it himself. It had never occurred to him to take a picture with the camera in his phone, but he decided that even with proof of what had happened, he was the only person on earth to whom it meant anything anyway.

When he had returned to the onion sacks, filled with shrimp and flounder earlier that morning, Baker had Jack Bailey in tow, but his wife and Christy were gone. His intentions had been to get the seafood taken care of right away, and Jack had offered to help. Instead, he was forced to look for the missing women.

Jack did indeed take care of the seafood, which freed up Baker to search for Sealy and Christy. He found the two in less than five minutes and was perplexed to find that Christy had talked his wife into calling 911 from the house of someone who lived several hundred yards down the shoreline. Both were now convinced that Jones would not have just disappeared like that.

At first Baker didn't think anything at all had happened to the old man, but the longer he listened to Sealy and Christy, the more plausible some disastrous possibility seemed to be. He got in touch with Jack by phone, and Jack calmed him down. Jack also canceled the rescue search.

Then, of course, Baker went right back to Sealy and Christy, listened to them talk, and was nervous all over again. With the seafood already gone, there was no reason for Baker not to join the girls on a search for the old man. And the longer they walked, the more conflicted he felt. Yes, Jones's history suggested the disappearance was merely part of a long-established pattern, but that pattern had been long established with someone else. Baker did not want to take any chances. Jones had helped him. He was one of the last people to see the old man. Baker felt responsible in some way. So, despite the absence of any kind of evidence that might have swayed opinion one way or another, Baker searched for Jones.

They had been walking north, up the bay's edge, for about ninety minutes with no sign of the old man, when the girls decided they needed water. Christy was not shy and said she would be happy to knock on a door and ask a stranger to save them from death by excessive thirst.

While the girls crossed a backyard and approached a woman on the porch, Baker stepped up onto the wharf and took several steps down it. He did not go far over the water's edge before stopping to look back in the direction from which they had come. His legs were spread widely, his feet firmly planted on the deck. Baker grabbed the railing and began to stretch a bit. He was stiff and sore from the activity of the previous night.

Glancing over his shoulder, he saw Sealy and Christy were still on the porch. The woman was not there, so he assumed she had gone inside to retrieve the requested water. When he turned back to resume stretching, Baker jumped and jerked his hands from the railing in alarm. While his attention had been directed toward the house, a bird had landed on the rail, only inches from his right hand.

Baker chuckled briefly and looked to the house again. He was the tiniest bit relieved to see that the two women had missed his reaction. The bird had scared him, and he had jumped almost completely across the wharf's walkway—a walkway that was not very wide at that point. Baker chuckled again as he got his breathing back under control and shook his head, somewhat embarrassed by his reaction to the small bird, which had been an arm-flailing jump more appropriate to a crocodile at one's feet. But the bird was very close to his hand, and he had always been nervous around birds anyway. And this one, despite Baker's crazy movement, had not left its spot on the rail.

"Okay, bird," Baker said aloud, "time to go." He flapped his hand at it, saying, "Go. Go! Shoo!" The bird merely cocked its head and hopped a couple of times. Baker placed his hands on his hips and frowned.

Baker had fished the bay and gulf most of his life and knew it was not unusual for a tired bird to stop and rest on one's boat or a wharf railing. Flying across the bay—why ever a bird did that in the first place—would tire the creatures. That is why, when the bird landed on the rail next to Baker, though he had been momentarily frightened, he was not surprised the bird had stopped to rest.

Baker crossed his arms. The bird didn't look tired to him. It occurred to him that birds rarely landed this close to humans on a wharf. When a boat was their only landing option, birds often would allow themselves to be picked up and held in one's hand. A wharf, though, has safer alternatives, since it is connected to shore, than the resting place this bird had chosen.

The bird flew a few feet from where it was and perched on the opposite rail, but it executed a sort of pause on the way, fluttering in Baker's face as if the man was in the way. Baker ducked and backed off a bit, totally flustered now and unsure whether to stand his ground or not.

When the bird began to vocalize with clacks and gulps and chortling pops and whirrs, Baker realized that the bird was a starling. He was fascinated, of course, having been significantly devastated by starlings, but he was curious to find that his rage had faded into an odd gratefulness to this species.

He and Sealy, the girls . . . they all were happier in the

apartment with the future they were planning than they had ever been in the much larger house. He had decided that boats and fishing and cooking gourmet meals at his own movable, outdoor restaurant appealed to him much more than farming ever did. Sealy was more excited than she had been in years. The flower bed business was already turning out to be a great idea for her, the family income, and their marriage.

The bird leaned toward Baker from the rail, screeching as if it were telling a story of its own to an audience of one. *Typical starling*, Baker thought. The bird was darkly colored but glistening with a shine accented by a speckled pattern. In the late morning sun, its glossy feathers, the blackest black, seemed polished by highlighted flecks of deep green.

The idea of gratefulness for a tough time had been rolling around Baker's thoughts for almost a week now. He had decided that had it not been for the starlings, he would not have met Jones. He was grateful for Jones, so Baker supposed that meant he was grateful for the starlings. After all, they were part of the process that brought Jones and him together.

Sealy had wondered aloud if Baker would have been open to a guy like Jones before—would Baker have really listened, she asked, had he not been in that awful position? Probably not, Baker had decided and, again, gave another point to the starlings.

Baker moved past the starling and leaned against then sat on the rail. The bird in front of him was jabbering incessantly. Baker thought of Jones at that moment and almost burst into tears. He was confused. Was he angry again? No, he didn't think so. And Jones was not hurt, was he? Or gone, right? Was it even possible, Baker mused, that he could have the terrible fortune to have finally found someone like the old man—a man who even called him "son"—only to be abandoned? Baker remembered Jones's often repeated words: *I'll be around. I always am.*

The bird's chattering increased. From Baker's vantage point its bright yellow beak contrasted with the background provided by the darker water of the bay. The bird was annoying, and Baker briefly considered attempting again to shoo the bird away but thought of Jones and did nothing.

Chattering, clicking, and whistling, the starling increased in volume. Baker looked up at the house and was dismayed to see that Sealy and Christy had evidently been invited inside, for they were nowhere in sight. He glanced at the bird. It seemed to be increasingly frantic, which struck Baker as funny. "What?" he said aloud to his guest and shook his head in amused wonder. Baker crossed his arms and peered at the house again. He wished Sealy would come outside just to see this ridiculous bird.

At that second the starling chose to stop chattering. From wide open, the bird went silent. It was such a sudden change that Baker jerked his head around to see what had happened. The bird jumped with a single flap of its wings and perched on Baker's left knee. Only a force of will kept the ex-farmer from toppling backward over the rail and into the water below.

Baker did not move, and for a moment, neither did the bird. The starling clicked once, made a gentle whirring sound, and slowly lifted its wings. Baker stared as the starling—this one, he knew, was a female—extended her wings to bare the feathers underneath.

The starling's open wings revealed an absence of speckles on their undersides. The feathers were jet black. Baker was transfixed; a gust of wind from nowhere, it seemed, blew down the length of the wharf. The starling leaned into the breeze as her feathers ruffled for a moment. Slowly, carefully folding her wings, the starling looked at Baker, shook herself once, and flew away.

Baker stood and shaded his eyes with a hand to watch her fly, twisting and looping through air currents and around obstacles imagined and real. It was so much like his own life, Baker thought. He, too, had generated some amazing twists and turns. Some of them had been good, some not so good. For a long time he had battled a tendency toward depression, and though Sealy did not know it, a couple of times he had even thought of suicide.

He had been happy. He had been sad. In his life Baker had experienced anger, fear, sorrow, love, longing, hate, defeat, joy, loss, and a hundred other feelings. Baker understood what hope felt like, and he knew the nagging ache of worry too. But never—not once until now—had Baker ever known what it was like to experience the peaceful calm of certainty.

He was overwhelmed, but in his mind and heart there was no longer any doubt that his life had meaning. He had purpose beyond himself, a purpose beyond today, beyond tomorrow . . . Beyond? Yes, he knew about that, too, for he had been given a glimpse of genuine truth.

A melody drifted across Baker's memory then . . . *What?* he thought. *What is that old song?* A line came to him quickly, and when it did, he sang it aloud: "His eye is on the sparrow, and I know He watches me . . ."

Baker smiled and looked to the sky. "Not just the sparrows," he murmured softly. "His eye is on the other birds too."

It was a genuine truth he would never forget. For Baker Larson had just seen a brilliant white spot under the wing of a starling.

Epilogue

S hortly after we talked to Christy and the Larsons, I left, having declined Jack's invitation to join him for lunch. It had occurred to me that I might look for Jones myself, but in any case, I knew I would not be good company. Frankly, despite my upbeat performance for our three new friends, I was sad.

As I thought about what I had told them about Jones and the situation, I had been satisfied that they were convinced about the old man's safety. On the other hand, I also recognized their longing, the strange sense of unfinished business, of things unsaid. They never had the opportunity to wrap Jones in their arms and express their gratitude. They never got to say, "I love you." There wasn't time to whisper good-bye.

I understood. I had been there. It was another of the lessons I had learned from him . . . a lesson he continued to teach. "Regret is tough to repair," he had said to me one night as we walked the beach. I was young, living under the pier, and still nursing wounds I carried from the deaths of my parents. "It's a fairly simple thing to avoid," he had said, "but regret surely is tough to repair."

"How do you avoid it?" I had asked, which I am certain was

what he had intended. "Really now, Jones . . . how can you avoid regret?"

"No unfinished business," he answered simply. "No good things left unsaid. Wrap folks in your arms. Express your gratitude. Always say, 'I love you.'" Then he shrugged. "That's how you avoid regret."

"Really?" I pushed him. "That's it?"

I will never forget . . . he stopped walking and turned to face me. "Yes, son," he said. "That's it. I thought you knew. But maybe you just don't want to think about it right now. One day you will. To avoid regret, you do and say and express every good thing you can possibly do and say and express to those you love. 'Cause you're going to find there isn't always time to whisper good-bye."

As I drove with the bay on my left, I wondered if I would ever become consistent in living my life with constant displays of gratitude. That's what I had decided it would take to live a life without personal regret even if there wasn't time to whisper good-bye.

Jones certainly seemed to disappear without my having told him how much he meant—to me and many other people. Every time the old man left—though I always looked and looked—I was unable to find him.

As the Fairhope Pier came into view on my left, I turned right and drove up the hill. At the top, I parked and looked carefully at the old house where I had learned so much just a few days before as Jones explained the beauty of "the first breath." Exiting the car, I walked into the yard and stood under the big oak tree. I remembered the feelings I had attempted to sort out the last time I was there. Now I was attempting to resolve a different kind of feeling.

As I considered the people I had met lately—those who had

also experienced more than a passing relationship with the old man—it seemed to me that their problems had been solved. Was I the only one in the group without an answer?

Christy had squealed in delight when Jack gave her the check for the seafood. It was, she told us over and over, exactly what she needed to buy the camera of her dreams. Baker and Sealy were also overjoyed with the financial windfall and were determined to begin their businesses without debt.

Jack and Mary Chandler were continually creating more ways to add value to the lives of those with whom they worked and lived. Bart and Kelli's lives, it appeared, had also taken on a new direction. Before leaving everyone at the bay, I had played a voice mail message from Bart, left on my cell phone. Would I be interested, he had asked excitedly, in attending their first parenting class? He and Kelli, he explained, would be teaching at the Eastern Shore Community Center, and thirty-one people were signed up so far. I had already called Polly, and we were making plans to be there together.

So was I the only one in the group without an answer to his life's most pressing problem? Apparently, yes, but I managed to chuckle, remembering that Jones would tell me it wasn't answers I needed. I needed perspective.

That was the moment, of course, when it hit me. I looked toward the house again and smiled broadly as the puzzle pieces in my head began to slide together. With a story of birth, Jones had explained death and in the process managed to remove much of the fear from the equation.

Jack had mentioned the huge perspective the old man had given Mary Chandler about Alzheimer's. I saw the opportunities created by thinking in a different manner. There were financial opportunities and opportunities to become the kind of parent or leader who would shape culture.

I shook my head and thought about Jones somewhere, walking along, laughing at me. He must have been amazed at my inability to see what was right in front of me. The truth, I now realized, was that everyday life, of which we all are a part, is exciting enough.

If I can manage to keep my eyes and ears open, a twenty-four-hour day holds undeniable drama, astounding possibilities, and the certainty of making a difference in the lives of others.

I remembered a remark Jones had made one night after I had complained about the condition of our nation and world. He had reminded me that we either create our culture or give in to the culture that already exists. Then he added, "See here, now . . . what's the first thing you do upon walking into a dark room? You flip the light switch, of course, and immediately the room is no longer dark.

"Light always trumps darkness. It always has, and it always will. Therefore," Jones said as his blue eyes bored into mine, "if you see that your world is darkening . . . if you believe that the culture of your nation is growing dimmer by the year . . . don't blame it on the dark! Darkness is only doing what darkness does.

"If darkness is winning the battles, my friend, it is because light is not doing its job. You are light. So wake up. Wake up." And then he said it again. "Wake up!"

As I walked away, I called Matt on my cell phone and told him my manuscript would be ready in seven days. I also warned him that there would not be some fantastic storyline with this one. No spies, no wars, no intrigue. This book would be a document of everyday life, and the book's hero would be an old man.

It is time to wake up, I thought.

I stood at my car and imagined Jones walking downhill to

the bay. In my mind he turned east there and finally walked out of sight a couple of minutes later. In fact, it was so clear that for a moment, I wasn't sure if I had imagined it or not.

As usual, there had not been time to whisper good-bye, but in my mind I wrapped my old friend tightly in my arms. I held him longer than he wanted, but I was able to express my gratitude and tell him how much I loved and appreciated him. It was an important moment for me. It was a connection that I needed and one that I felt deeply.

And, of course, I wanted to get everything said, for in truth, I didn't know exactly when I would see the old man again. Not that I was worried about it. I knew Jones would be around if I needed him.

He always was.

Acknowledgments

If you have ever heard me talk about a book I have released, I almost always use "we" instead of "I." As in, *we* just released *The Noticer Returns*. Believe it or not, I don't talk like that because I have multiple personalities. The reality is, without the support of the friends and family who make up my team, none of this would be possible. Everything *I* do is actually part of a much larger *we* effort. The following people are those who make up the *we*. Thank you all for your presence in my life:

Polly, my wife and best friend. Thanks for your love, wit, patience, and happy spirit.

Austin and Adam, our boys. You guys are the best. I am so proud of who you are becoming. Remember to smile while you talk!

Robert D. Smith, my personal manager and champion. After thirty-four years together, you still manage to make every day count.

Todd Rainsberger. Your "story" advice is always on the mark.

Scott Jeffrey. Your guidance and wisdom have kept us steered in the right direction for years.

Duane Ward and the entire team at Premiere Speakers Bureau. We have become such great friends that I often forget we are partners.

Gail and Mike Hyatt, one of the best couples I know. Had it not been for you, this book would probably not exist.

Matt Baugher, my publisher from W. Your wisdom is exceeded only by your patience. In addition to being the best at what you do, you have become a great friend.

Paula Major, my editor, whose careful eye and discerning mind made this a much better book.

Emily Sweeney, Stephanie Newton, Kristi Smith, Tom Knight, Big Jeff Miller, and the dozens of people at W who helped get this book into the hands of as many people as possible.

Kurt V. Beasley and Brent C. Gray, who handle the legal rights to all my intellectual property.

Sandi Dorff, Paula Tebbe, Susie White, and Tommie McGaster, who direct the daily parts of my life. Without the effort, prayer, and attention to detail of these four people, my own efforts would not come to nearly so much.

Kristi and Steve Woods, my sister and brother-in-law. Our whole family is grateful for your presence in our lives.

Paul "Saul" Fries, Matt Lempert, Chase Neely, Keith Misner, Kyle Martin, Brandon Triola, David Loy, and Will Hoekenga, for their amazing behind-the-scenes work in the Nashville office.

Peggy Hoekenga, for developing fantastic curriculum for this book and all the others.

The Isaacs: Lily, Becky, Sonya, and Ben. Your music is a constant presence in our home.

A very special thank you to Patsy Clairmont, my favorite tiny person. My two years speaking in arenas with you were the most fun I have ever had on stage. And while watching you speak, I took the most notes I have ever taken anywhere. Thanks for your influence and example.

Thank you also to Shannon and John Smith, for allowing me to write in your house down the street on the many occasions that my own house was too noisy.

And to Katrina and Jerry Anderson, Mary Louise and Wil Baker, Vicki and Brian Bakken, Bob Bolen, Sunny Brownlee, Foncie and Joe Bullard, Kayla Carter, Jennifer R. Casebier, Kelly and David Cleere, Robin and Scott Coleman, Diane and Tony DiLeonardi, Gloria and Bill Gaither, Michelle and Brian Gibbons, Gloria and Martin Gonzalez, Bill Gothard, Donna and Art Holmes, Jennifer and Dave Hooten, Lynn and Mike Jakubik, Brian C. Johnson, Kent Kirby, Deb and Gilbert Little, Nancy Lopez, Mark Lowry, Melanie and Mike Martin, Karen and Alan McBride, Liz and Bob McEwen, Edna McLoyd, Martis Overstreet, Mary and Jim Pace, Glenda and Kevin Perkins, Brenda and Todd Rainsberger, Sharon and Dave Ramsey, Becky and Ted Romano, Barbara Selvey, Claudia and Pat Simpson, Jean and Sandy Stimpson, Dr. Christopher Surek, Maryann and Jerry Tyler, Mary Ann and Dave Winck, Sherry and Richard Wright, and Kathy and Mike Wooley. Your influence in my life is undeniable, and your example is very much appreciated.

CONTACT ANDY

To interact with Andy through
Facebook and Twitter, visit

AndyAndrews.com

Teachers, don't forget to download your
free companion curriculum at

AndyAndrews.com/Education

To book Andy for corporate events, call

(800) 726-ANDY (2639)

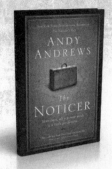

The
NOTICER

*Sometimes, all a person needs
is a little perspective.*

ISBN: 978-0-7852-2921-6

*"The Noticer is completely absorbing. Anything less
than stunning would be an understatement. This is
not just one of the best books I have read . . . This is
the best book I have ever read in my life."*

NANCY LOPEZ,
LPGA HALL OF FAMER

THE
BUTTERFLY
EFFECT

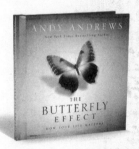

HOW YOUR LIFE MATTERS

ISBN: 978-1-4041-8780-1

*"Every single thing you do matters.
You have been created as one of a kind.
You have been created in order to make a difference.
You have within you the power to change the world."*

ANDY ANDREWS